OLD HOMES AND FAMILIES
IN NOTTOWAY

By

W. R. TURNER

CLEARFIELD

Originally published
Blackstone, Virginia, 1932

Reprinted for
Clearfield Company, Inc by
Genealogical Publishing Co , Inc
Baltimore, Maryland
1998

International Standard Book Number: 0-8063-4789-9

Made in the United States of America

To My Daughters
VIRGINIA READ
and
MARY HOLCOMBE

NOTTOWAY COURT HOUSE

The scene of many court days, political meetings and stirring
events (Page 62)

CONTENTS

ERRATA

In Contents—Walnut Hill—**McHenry,** should read, **McEnery.**
Page 80—**IVERNESS** should read **INVERNESS.**

ILLUSTRATIONS

FOREWORD

The author of this little volume wishes it clearly understood that in no sense does he intend it to be a history of Nottoway County, but rather, a collection of notes gathered by him from time to time, and recorded here for the use of any who may be interested in the families and homes of our county.

May this effort inspire some loyal son or daughter of Nottoway at some not far distant day, to weave into a finished history of the county these notes and those of Hon. Walter A. Watson, whose untimely death cut short the task he had hoped to accomplish, for which he collected much material, and for which he was so admirably fitted.

It may be remarked that the writer has gone into more detail concerning some families than others, which would seem to indicate a greater interest on his part in these particular families. This is not the case, however, but is due to a lack of available data in some instances, and not to any intentional oversight.

We wish to express our grateful thanks and appreciation to those who so kindly furnished us their records and data, without which, this work could not have been accomplished.

THE FOLLOWING BOOKS WERE USED AS REFERENCES

"Notes on Southside Virginia" by Hon. Walter A. Watson.

"Rev. William S. White and His Times" by Rev. H. M. White.

"History of the Nottoway Grays" by Captain Richard Irby.

"The Borderland in the Civil War" by Edward Conrad Smith.

"The Life and Character of Edwin Gilliam Booth" by Harry E. Dwight, M. D., D. D.

"Howe's History of Virginia."

"Martin's Gazetteer of Virginia."

The County Records of Nottoway, Amelia, Lunenburg, Prince George and Surry counties.

W. R. Turner
March, 1932

OLD HOMES AND FAMILIES IN NOTTOWAY

The period between the close of the Revolutionary War in 1781, and the beginning of the Civil War in 1861, was the golden age in Virginia. Especially was this true of Nottoway and the Southside. This section being predominantly agricultural, the large plantation was the rule. Here was the stronghold of slavery, and here perhaps slavery wore its kindliest aspect.

The planter had time to cultivate the elegancies of life, to engage much in social intercourse, and to become familiar with all current political topics. Consequently it was during this period that Virginia produced many of her greatest men, and from this system, there arose that hospitality for which her people were noted. Nowhere were the wishes and wants of the guest more regarded, and nowhere was the character of a true gentleman held more sacred. No people had a clearer sense of honor nor higher regard for womankind.

Dr. Wm. S. White, a noted Presbyterian Divine who served the people of Nottoway for some years during this time, says in his book, "Dr. Wm. S. White and His Times", "My life in Nottoway may be characterized as one of incessant but delightful labor. That county had long been celebrated for the politeness, refinement, and hospitality of its inhabitants. But they were deplorably irreligious. Card playing, horse racing and wine drinking were almost universal among the higher classes." Then came the War Between the

States. The people of Nottoway responding nobly both in men and means, made a record during this period too well known to be recorded here. Suffice it to say the county furnished five Companies to the Confederate cause. Co. G the 18th Virginia, "The Nottoway Grays." Co. C the 18th Virginia, "The Nottoway Rifle Guards." Co. E the 3rd Virginia, "The Nottoway Cavalry." Jeffress Battery and the Nottoway Reserves. Pickett's Division was recruited largely from this and adjoining counties.

The Nottoway Grays in Pickett's immortal charge at the battle of Gettysburg had only six men left who were not killed, wounded or captured, and Richard Ferguson, a member of the Company and adjutant of the Regiment, was captured beyond the stone wall.

Being removed from the scene of the conflict, Nottoway's soil suffered little from the invading armies. However, on June 23rd, 1864, "The Grove" was the scene of a battle between the Union raiders, Kautz and Wilson, and General W. H. F. Lee, in which the raiders were driven back. Later the retreating and conquering armies passed through her borders only a few days before the end at Appomattox.

Then came the surrender and reconstruction, and with the people there followed a struggle for existence and a fight with poverty for years thereafter.

Their State had now a tyrant's heel upon her neck and was called Military District Number One, a conquered province. Military satraps filled the seats of judges and magistrates, and the ignorant slave was often shown more deference than his former master. Even through all this the old customs and manners persisted—the same courtesy, the same high sense of honor, and the same hospitality.

In Nottoway for the most part, after the war and even as late as the early years of the present century, the old plantations were the homes of families who had owned them for generations. This is not the case today, for changing economic conditions have forced them to sell or rent their lands, and few estates are now in the hands of those who possessed them a generation ago.

A home was worthy of a name in those days, and it is to preserve the names of some of these old homes and families of a past generation that this effort is made.

SCHWARTZ TAVERN: In Blackstone stands an old house, now the home of Gilliam Anderson. One looks with interest at its secret stairway and shudders as he sees the blood stains on the floor and hears the story of the gruesome murder which tradition says took place here.

It seems that a man lived here, his name has passed with the years, who had a beautiful daughter. Like all beautiful daughters, she fell in love, but unfortunately her suitor did not meet with the approval of her father, who forbade the young man paying her further attentions.

One night the lovers decided to elope. About midnight, the girl attired in her best silk dress, started down the stairs to meet her sweetheart. The rustling of the silk dress and the creaking of the stairs awoke the father, who, rushing to the scene, beat the young man to death. It is said that often now about mid-night one can hear the rustling of a silk dress and the creaking of the stairs, followed by blows, and then groans, as the awful scene is being re-enacted.

This old house was formerly a tavern. Just ten years after the surrender of Cornwallis, John A. Schwartz, a German, acquired the tavern property from Jemima Williams, widow of James Williams, who built the house. James Williams bought the land from a Mr. Cocke.

Schwartz, a year previous to this time, had bought from Peter Randolph, who was the second clerk of Nottoway County, later judge, and still later Judge of the Superior Court, a tract of land nearby. Across the road, Jordan's Road, from the Schwartz tavern stood an older tavern run by Francis White, and the settlement which soon sprang up around them became known as Blacks and Whites from the two tavern owners. It will be recalled that Schwartz is the German word for black.

About 1885 the citizens thought a more dignified name should be chosen, and decided to call the place Bellefonte. This met with some opposition from the Post Office Department, there being other places by the same name. Finally, at the suggestion of Dr. J. M. Hurt, the name Blackstone was chosen, after the famous English jurist of that name.

A short distance east of Blackstone was another settlement called New Blacks and Whites, where, according to the late R. W. Sydnor, Court was held for a time before the Court House was permanently located.

HAMLIN'S TAVERN stood just west of Blackstone, the first tavern built in the lower end of Nottoway County, and was located on the north side of Jordan's (now Hungary Town) road. There are no records to indicate when it was built, but it stood in great dilapidation as late as 1787. The house now occupied by E. M. Jones is only a few yards east of the tavern site, and across the road to the south a straight double race track ran for a quarter of a mile. The race paths, overgrown with brush and trees, may still be seen on the south side of the road. Almost opposite the tavern stood "Southern Chapple" or Green's Church, built about 1740. On October 28, 1740, the Vestry of Bristol Parish ordered "that the Southern Chapple be built at the Hurricane nearest the best water." Green's Church was one of the first Episcopal churches in this section. Here services were held for a number of years until the rector, Parson Wilkerson, who had married in this country, was unfortunate enough to have a former wife from England appear on the scene. This caused such consternation in his flock that further services were abandoned. The Presbyterians later used the old building for their worship until it was burned about 1827. The site of this old church is now occupied by the house of Pryor Jones.

OAKWELL: Leaving Blackstone by the Cryers or Darville road, we soon come to Oakwell, built by Archer Worsham about 1840. Later Dr. T. W. Sydnor, a Baptist Minister, who preached in this and surrounding counties for forty-two years, lived here. He married Blanche McClanahan. After Dr. Sydnor's death, his son, R. W. Sydnor, lived here. R. W. Sydnor served in the Confederate Army as captain of the Nottoway Reserves. He married Mary Lilly Cook.

SHENSTONE is a short distance from Oakwell, and before the war was the home of Edwin Booth.

The house was probably built by his father, Gilliam Booth, whose wife was Rebecca Hicks.

Edwin Booth was born at Shenstone January 11, 1810. On his maternal side, his grandfather, Colonel Hicks was a prominent officer of the Revolution. He was educated at the University of North Carolina and later studied law under Judge Taylor Lomax, professor at the University of Virginia and Judge of the Court of Appeals. Later finishing his law course, he began the practice of law in Nottoway and the adjacent counties, and rapidly rose to the top in his profession. In 1874 he was elected to the Virginia Legislature, and in 1849 was selected by that body among other prominent members to revise the code of Virginia. Later he was prominently mentioned for the governorship. In the campaign preceding the war, Edwin Booth, a staunch Whig, supported Bell and Everett. He married in the autumn of 1833 Sally Tanner Jones, a descendant of Peter Jones, for whom Petersburg was named. She died just before the outbreak of the war.

In 1863 Mr. Booth married Henrietta Chauncey, the daughter of Elihu Chauncey, a wealthy citizen of Philadelphia. In order to make the trip to Philadelphia at that time, it was necessary to pass through the blockade, and Mr. Booth received a permit from President Lincoln himself, which insured him a safe journey. Just before leaving for Philadelphia, Mr. Booth took breakfast with President Jefferson Davis in Richmond, and in less than a month, when he passed through Wash-

SCHWARTZ TAVERN
Now the Anderson home.

ington on his way to Philadelphia, he dined with President Lincoln at the White House. To have been entertained by the two Presidents was a distinction probably accorded no other private citizen.

While in the North during the later years of the war, Mr. Booth did much for his friends who were in prison in securing comforts for them, and in some cases, their parole. After the war he purchased Carter's Grove on the James River. He died in February 1886 in his seventy-seventh year. Edwin Booth had five children by his first marriage, all of whom died before their father, except one son, Dr. Edwin G. Booth. A son, Archer Jones Booth, a member of Company E, the Nottoway Cavalry, was killed at Mount Jackson during the war.

Dr. Edwin G. Booth, a son of Edwin Booth, married Clara Haxall Thompson of Jefferson County, West Virginia, and next lived at Shenstone. Dr. Booth was a member of Company G, the Nottoway Grays, and was later transferred to the Confederate Navy as surgeon on board the "Selma". His ship took a prominent part in the battle of Mobile Bay, where after a fierce fight against overwhelming odds, the Confederate fleet, under Admiral Buchanan, was defeated.

Dr. Booth, along with Admiral Buchanan and others, was taken prisoner, and sent to Pensacola, Florida, where he was released on parole. Soon afterwards, the war closed, and Dr. Booth returned to Shenstone to live. He did much for the Democratic party in holding it together during Reconstruction times and served as chairman of the party in the county for many years. He later moved to Carter's Grove, on the James River. After a time he sold Carter's Grove, and returned to Nottoway. Finally he moved to Williamsburg and died January 5, 1922, in the Wythe House. Dr. Booth had seven children, four daughters and three sons. His daughter, Lucy, married Dr. Hugh S. Cumming, Surgeon-General of the United States under three Presidents. Another daughter, Henrietta, married Henry S. Wise, and Fannie married James A. Ballantine, of San Francisco, California.

A son, William Harris Booth, a lieutenant commander in the United States Navy, now retired, married Hilda Millet of Boston. His son, Edwin Booth, of New York, married Edith Thompson of Atlanta, Georgia. Another son, Thompson Booth, a physician, married Conde Bridges of Ashland, Virginia, and a daughter, Clara Booth, never married.

THE RETREAT is not far from Shenstone on the Blackface road. Dr. Sydnor, who lived at Oakwell, bought the place during the war for his brother's family to refugee here; hence the name, The Retreat. Dr. Connalley lived here once, as did Dr. Blandy, who married Mary Jane Booth, a niece of Edwin Booth of Shenstone. Dr. Blandy came to Nottoway from Delaware, which was a slave State at that time, and his sympathies were entirely Southern. He was surgeon of Company G, the Nottoway Grays, and was detailed after the battle of Gettysburg to take charge of the hospital located at Blacks and Whites, near where the Norfolk and Western Depot now stands. He was later transferred to Burkeville where a large hospital was operated during the latter part of the war. In later years Captain Taylor, an Englishman and a bachelor who lived the life of a hermit, made his home at The Retreat.

NORBORN HILL, five or six miles from The Retreat was the home of Major Robert Neblett, whose wife was Mary Eliza Gilliam. All that is left of this old home are three enormous chimneys, twelve feet across, which bear witness to the fine old mansion that was. Before it burned, it was the home of E. B. Maddux, whose wife was Lucy Bagley. Major Robert Neblett was a great nephew of Nathaniel Neblett of Haymarket. He had three children: Eliza, who married Carter Haskins; Mary Anna, who never married, and John, who married Emily Rives.

HAYMARKET, on Nottoway River a short distance away, was the home of Nathaniel Neblett, a veteran of the War of 1812. Nathaniel Neblett was the son of Sterling Neblett and Mary Chappell of Woodlawn, in Lunenburg County. He married Elizabeth Davis, nee Fisher, widow of Ashley Davis, and had the following children: Eliza, Rebecca and Anne. Eliza married Charles Smith, treasurer of Lunenburg County. Anne married Dr. W. H. Perry of Lunenburg, and Rebecca died unmarried. Nathaniel Neblett died in 1816.

Just before the Civil War, Dr. Reps Connalley, a son of William Connalley and Rebecca Ledford Jones, bought Haymarket, rebuilt the house, and lived here for a number of years. Dr. Connalley married Sallie Fletcher Jones, January 9, 1865, a daughter of Captain Richard Jones of Bellefonte. Dr. Connalley was the first captain of the Nottoway Grays. He was a physician of note and was graduated from Jefferson Medical College in Philadelphia March 29, 1848. He had a large family of children. Dr. Connalley died December 20, 1870.

BELLEFONTE is a short distance east of Blackstone. Near here was a race track, famous in the old times, run by Colonel Jeter and laid off about the year 1822. This was the rendezvous of the Bellefonte Jockey Club. Says Dr. White in his book: "The wealth, style, and beauty of Old Virginia assembled here from time to time. All the distinguished racers attended, coming from the Blue Ridge on the West to the Chesapeake Bay on the East and North Carolina line on the South." Wm. R. Johnston of North Carolina "King of Turf" often attended, as did Captain Jimmie Junkin Harrison of Diamond Grove, in Brunswick County, John R. Goode of Mecklenburg, Colonel William Wynn of Petersburg, John Randolph of Roanoke and others. Many days were spent in the most exciting forms of fashionable dissipation, such as cards, wine, balls and betting on the races. The American Turf Register and Sporting Magazine of Baltimore, Maryland, for August 1833 gives an account of the Spring Meeting at Bellefonte which commenced on May 29th. Major Hezekiah Anderson was president of the club at one time, and Captain Richard Jones owner. The popularity of this resort began to decline under the combined preaching of the different ministers in the county. Major Anderson and Captain Richard Jones both joined the church and the large hotel or tavern was afterwards turned into a seminary for young ladies. Colonel Jeter became a bankrupt and died in a small cabin across from Bellefonte near where the Greenhill road comes into Cocke's road.

Captain Richard Jones married Elizabeth Epes, daughter of Major John Epes, November 17, 1818, and made his home here after the Bellefonte race track was abandoned.

Captain John E. Jones, a son of Captain Richard Jones, who married Sarah Bouldin, also lived here. He was captain of Company E, Nottoway Cavalry.

MORGANSVILLE, an old settlement a short distance from Bellefonte, formerly called Edmondson's Old Ordinary, was burned by Tarleton's Cavalry during the Revolutionary War in the raid in which they captured Peter Francisco. After this it was known as Burnt Ordinary and was later purchased from John McRae of Petersburg by Captain Samuel Morgan, who married Lucy Wills April 14th, 1791. Captain Morgan was the son of John Morgan and Amy Wilson, and his wife was the daughter of Lawrence Wills and Anne Pryor. Their children were Amy A., who married Meriwether Hurt; Mary H., who married a Jackson; Lucy, who married a Bridgforth; Catherine, who married a Reese; Samuel W., Jr., and John L.

Captain Morgan named the place Morgansville and ran a tavern, store and post-office, one of the first post offices in the county. Though a slave owner himself, like many other slave owners of his time, he was opposed to the institution of slavery.

On one of his many business trips to New York City, he wrote home to his wife on February 21st, 1831, "I feel proud that I have this opportunity of putting my foot in a State where the shocking shame of slavery does not exist." It is interesting also to note that in the same letter he said of our metropolis, "New York is a thriving city of two hundred and seven thousand souls, far superior to any city in America". With the advent of the fashionable resort at Bellefonte, Captain Morgan's business began to decline.

He hit upon a novel way to get ahead of his rival, Colonel Jeter, and made the following proposition to the Presbyterian Minister, Dr. White. Said he: "On that part of my land which borders on Jeter's race track, there is a beautiful site for a church. If you will place your building there, I will give you an acre of ground, covered with a beautiful grove of oaks, and I will give you besides fifty dollars in money". This offer was gladly accepted, and Shiloh Church was built in 1828 in accordance with the old Captain's wish. Some people were unkind enough to question the old man's motives in donating the site for the church, but Dr. White never did. He said of him, "The Captain did not sell spirituous liquors and hated card playing and horse racing."

PELION HILL is a short distance across the road from Morgansville, named, no doubt, after Pelion in Grecian Mythology, in which the sons of Aloeus, renowned for their strength and courage, attempted by piling Ossa upon Pelion, to scale Olympus and dethrone the immortals. They were stopped only when Jupiter himself slew them with his lightning.

Dr. Blandy, whose wife was Mary Jane Booth, lived here at one time, and in 1859 he sold the place to Rainelle Beville, who married Lizzy Clotty. When Rainelle Beville died, his son, Archer Beville, who married Sarah Clay, inherited the property and has since lived here.

ASPEN GROVE is just south of Wellville. This was built by Wood Jones, who married Miss Wilson. Wood Jones was the county surveyor. He recommended the present site for the Court House, as this location is near the center of the county as prescribed by the acts of the legislature cutting Nottoway off from Amelia in 1788. His son, John Wood Jones, who has recently passed away, served in Jeffress Battery during the Civil War, and was probably the last of his company.

EPESTON on the Greenhill road not far from Bellefonte was the home of Dr. William Jordan Harris, a native of Powhatan County, whose wife was Helen Epes, and in honor of whom he named his home. He studied at the University of Virginia, was graduated from the Jefferson Medical College in Philadelphia, and was a member of the first examining board of the State of Virginia. One of his papers on pneumonia was read before the London Medical Society, and he is said to have been the first physician to establish the relationship between skin and throat diphtheria. His two sons, Major Peter Epes Harris and Captain James Madison Harris, who did much for their day and generation, were both born at Epeston. Another son, Richard Herbert Harris, a brilliant young doctor, died in early manhood.

Captain Harris said, "Just after General Lee surrendered a large body of Union soldiers were camped between Epeston and Bellefonte. I was a young boy and enjoyed seeing them drill and hearing the bands play. Soon came the news of Lincoln's assassination, and my father, Dr. Harris, apprehensive lest the troops would be incensed by the news and commit some act of vandalism, applied to the commanding officer for a guard. This request was readily granted. His fears were unfounded, however, as the soldiers were not at all excited by the news, and their remarks about the dead President were anything but complimentary." It would seem from this that Mr. Lincoln at the time of his death was not popular, even with the army.

ABBEVILLE, the seat of the Blands in Nottoway, was settled by Edward Bland, son of Peter Bland of Jordan's Point, Prince George County, who came to Nottoway and applied for a license to practice law in 1794. His wife was Rebecca Jones, daughter of Batte Jones of Falkland in Nottoway.

Edward Bland's son, William Richard Bland, was a strong Whig and one of the members of the first agricultural club organized in Nottoway. He was a prominent lawyer and was married twice. His first wife was Betty Irby, daughter of William Blunt Irby, and his second was Matilda Epes. He moved from Abbeville to Springfield nearby, which was a Bland quarter settlement, and died there.

Edward Bland, who settled in Nottoway, was a direct descendant of the Theoderick Bland who established the estate of Westover on the James River where he is buried.

Theoderick Bland's wife was Anne Bennett, daughter of Richard Bennett, governor of the colony. Theoderick's son, Richard I, moved to Jordan's Point in Prince George County and was married twice. His first wife was Mary whose last name is not known. His second was Elizabeth Randolph, daughter of Colonel William Randolph of Turkey Island. By this marriage he had a large family.

Richard II, son of Richard I, married Anne Poythress. He was a man of great intellect, was called the "Virginia Antiquary" and was a political writer of note. He wrote "Letters to the Clergy", and "An Inquiry into the Rights of the Colonies", and was a member of the First Continental Congress. Mr. Jefferson pronounced him "the wisest man south of the James River."

Richard II's son, Peter Bland, married Judith Booker, and it was their son, Edward, who settled at Abbeville in Nottoway. Thomas W. Epes, nicknamed "Dodger", who married Miss Williams, lived at Abbeville in later years.

CENTERVILLE was another Bland settlement. John Bland lived here, whose first wife was Miss Jones, a daughter of Batte Jones of Falkland and whose second wife was Polly Perkinson. The children by the last marriage were George Bland of Greenhill and Thomas Bland of The Grove. John Bland once owned Doolittle. At one time Richard Epes (Clerk) Dick who married Agnes Batte, lived at Centerville.

DOOLITTLE, farther along the Greenhill road, was the home of B. D. M. Jones, who was considered at one time the richest man in Nottoway County. He was a man of education, a Harvard graduate. His wife was Virginia Scott, a sister of Anderson Scott, of Oak Hill. Isaac Epes who married Rosalie Beverley, once lived here and sold the place to B. D. M. Jones for fifty thousand dollars.

THE ACRE, the home of the Shores, was settled by Dr. Edwin Shore, who is said to have moved to Nottoway and bought an acre of land; hence the name of his home, The Acre. He was a prominent physician, and his practice grew as well as his acres. He married twice: his first wife was Epes Ward, and the second, the widow, Anne Scott, nee Epes. His daughter, Anne Shore, married Freeman Fitzgerald, and they lived at **Claremont,** about two miles north of J. A. Clay's store, while his son, Valley Shore, married Sallie Ward and lived at Gilliams, not far from The Acre.

GREENHILL, the home of Colonel William C. Greenhill, who married Miss Claiborne, was near where Clay's store now stands.

He was the Colonel Greenhill who figured so prominently in the Bacon-Hardaway duel which terminated in the death of Dr. Hardaway. Strange to say, the principals in this affair did not fight. An account of this unfortunate duel, which occurred in July 1818, is set forth in Notes on Southside Virginia by Hon. Walter A. Watson, and is in part as follows:

"Colonel William C. Greenhill and Colonel Tyree G. Bacon were prominent citizens of Nottoway. Greenhill lived in the lower end of the county, I think, at a place called Greenhill on Sellar Creek. He was a man of education. Colonel Greenhill, and Colonel Bacon, who had been a delegate in the legislature, had some personal or political differences, it seems. Randolph, when elected Judge of the General Court, about 1812, was colonel of the Militia regiment, and Bacon was the major. To the vacancy, Greenhill, a cousin of Randolph, was elected by the officers of the regiment, being promoted over the head of Bacon. This was probably the beginning of the feud which led to the unfortunate affair."

Colonel Bacon's son, Dr. Bacon, was at the time living in Mecklenburg County. Dr. John S. Hardaway, being unaware of the nature of the communication, bore the challenge from Colonel Greenhill to Colonel Bacon. Colonel Bacon placed the blame on Dr. Hardaway. Dr. Bacon and Dr. Hardaway met at Nottoway Court House afterwards, and staged a stabbing match, in which Dr. Hardaway was mortally wounded. The fight took place just at the gate on the path leading from the Court House to the old tavern. Dr. Hardaway lived one or two days after the duel and died in the Jackson house lately occupied by John B. Tuggle. Dr. Bacon was tried but acquitted.

Before the Bacon-Hardaway duel, Colonel Greenhill was shot and dangerously wounded on May 29, 1816, by Captain Thomas Wells as he and Judge Randolph were entering the tavern yard at Nottoway Court House. Judge Randolph was also wounded, but recovered, as did Colonel Greenhill. Wells was tried but acquitted, and later went to Georgia, where he was subsequently hanged for murder in that State.

In later years George Bland, who married Rebecca Straghan, lived at Greenhill. Their children were Blackwell, George, Dora, who married a Miller; Janet, who married Mr. Townsend, and Mellville.

SILENT SHADES was the home of Richard Osborne. He married Sarah Epes whose home was at **Bloomfield** near by. Dick Osborne served in the Civil War as a member of Company E, 3rd Virginia Cavalry. He was a great fox hunter, and always kept a large pack of hounds. When Bloomfield burned in 1875, the widow Epes and her daughters, Georgiana, Fanny, Sarah and Ellen, who lived there, were invited to share the hospitality of Silent Shades, and they accepted the invitation. This was the beginning of the romance which later developed into the marriage of Richard Osborne and Sarah Epes.

THE GROVE was another Bland settlement farther on the Greenhill road and near Deep Creek. Thomas Bland, who married a Miss Worsham, lived here. Their daughter, Mollie Beck, married Captain William E. Hinton, and another daughter, Ella, married Dr. Olando Hinton, a brother of William E. Hinton. Captain William E. Hinton later lived at The Grove in the summer making his home in Petersburg in the winter.

FANCY HILL is not far from Silent Shades and was the home of Colonel Travis Epes, whose wife was Elizabeth Branch Jones. Colonel Epes was a son of Major John Epes and Frances Campbell Epes, and a grandson of Colonel Francis Epes, Jr., who first settled in Nottoway.

Colonel Travis Harris Epes, who was an outstanding man in his time, was a staunch Whig and violently opposed to secession.

He served in the Virginia Legislature 1833-34, and during the presidential campaign preceding the Civil War he was unceasing in his efforts in behalf of Bell and Everett, the Constitutional Union candidates, who believed in the Union, but did not believe in coercion.

After Virginia seceded, however, he gave unstintingly of his resources to his State, and four of his sons served in the Confederate Army. He took a prominent part in the meeting held at Nottoway Court House April 7th, 1861, to decide on secession, and at that meeting stood almost alone in opposition to Virginia's leaving the Union. He was the father of Judge Branch Epes of Gatewood in Dinwiddie County, a captain of Artillery in the Confederate States Army.

OAK HILL. Dr. William S. White, the Presbyterian minister whom Dr. Pryor succeeded, lived here once, and later on it was the home of Anderson Scott, whose wife was Charlotte Wilsie. After the battle of The Grove, Oak Hill was used as a Confederate hospital.

Captain John K. Jones, whose wife was Edmonia Field, once lived at Oak Hill. He was captain of Company E, 3rd Virginia Cavalry.

TURKEY ISLAND, not far from Oak Hill, was thought to have been owned by Hamlin Harris. It was later a Dickinson settlement, and was afterwards owned by Colonel Calvin Jeffress. In this neighborhood are **Red Hill,** owned by Archer Cralle, and **Cheathams,** owned by Dr. Algie Epes. A great many Indian relics are to be found near here at a place called **Caskies,** indicating that is was once a trading post with the Indians.

FALKLAND, one of the oldest homes in this section, was built by Batte Jones, before the Revolutionary War. Batte Jones, a descendant of Peter Jones, who established Peter's Point, married Margaret Ward. Their son, Peter Branch Jones, who married Martha Epes, lived here also, and later Hamlin Epes, a son of Colonel Travis Epes, made it his home. Hamlin Epes was color bearer of Company E, 3rd Virginia Cavalry.

RURAL RETREAT is on the Cottage road, formerly known as Irby's road. It was the home of G. Truly Cralle, who married Elizabeth Gilliam Willson, of Amelia County. Truly Cralle served in Company E, 3rd Virginia Cavalry during the Civil War.

His son, Colonel G. Maury Cralle, has had a long and honorable career in the United States Army. He was graduated from West Point in 1898 to enter the Spanish-American War, and served during that war in Cuba, later he served in the Philippine Islands, and still later in Alaska. At one time he was Quarter Master General for the Canal Zone. Soon after the outbreak of the World War he was stationed at Camp Logan, Texas, where he trained the 79th Infantry. After the Armistice, he was assigned to Governors Island. His last assignment was Commandant of Alcatraz Prison off the coast of California. He made such a notable record here in the management of the prison, by establishing new industries for the prisoners and in rehabilitation that he attracted national attention. Alcatraz was considered a model prison in every respect under his management. He is now retired and lives in Washington, D. C.

WINDROW, a short distance from Rural Retreat, is so named on account of its having been in the path of a terrible wind storm which uprooted many trees, but which fortunately did not cover

FANCY HILL

Once the home of Colonel Travis Epes

a very wide area. It was of such violence, however, that one of the overseer's small children was blown several miles away, where it was found dead after the storm. Isaac Holmes, who was the first clerk of Nottoway County, 1788 to 1793, lived here, and the first deputy Clerk's office in the county was located in a house in the yard. Windrow was once owned by Captain Richard Jones, and there is an old Jones burying ground at this place. Mrs. Crawley Jones was the last of the Jones family buried here. Richard Jones sold the place to Rev. Theodorick Pryor, who sold it to his brother-in-law, Thomas Freeman Epes, about 1839, who lived here until a good many years after the Civil War. He was the son of Major John Epes and Frances Campbell Epes, and a grandson of Colonel Francis Epes, Jr., who first settled in Nottoway. He married twice; his first wife was Jacqueline Segar Hardaway, and his second Rebecca Dupuy.

Unlike his brother, Colonel Travis Epes, of Fancy Hill, Thomas Freeman Epes was a Democrat and an ardent secessionist. Although he himself was too old to serve in the army, several of his sons served in the war with distinction.

Many stories are told about the quaint characteristics of Thomas Freeman Epes. He was a great lover of fox hunting, and kept one of the best packs of hounds in the county, following the sport even in his old age. He kept, for a number of years, a diary of all his hunts, and could tell just how the fox ran on any particular day. He knew just how many foxes he caught each season. During the period of ten years from 1866-67 to 1876-77 he caught three hundred and fifty-two, an average of 35.2 foxes per season, about one third of this number being reds.

But woe unto the one who incurred his displeasure during the hunt or took issue with him concerning the chase!

On one occasion he was hunting with a party of friends. The chase had been a long one, finally losing the run on the fox altogether. Passing a sandy place in the road, he said to his grandson, who was with him, "Get down there, sir, and see if there are any fox tracks in the sand." The youngster obeyed, but being tired, he made the fatal mistake of first looking up at the sun to see what time it was, whereupon the old gentleman roared, "You little fool, don't you know there are no fox tracks up in the sky"!

In his home, however, he was the typical old-fashioned Virginia gentleman, hospitable to a fault—nothing was too good for his guests, nor could their stay be too prolonged.

His son, Dr. Theodorick Pryor Epes, whose wife, Joanna Tyler Spencer, a great, great, granddaughter of Jack Jouett, of Revolutionary fame, and a granddaughter of James Wood Bouldin at one time a member of Congress, was a Presbyterian minister greatly beloved by the people of Nottoway, whom he served for twenty years. Dr. Epes received his A. B. degree from Washington and Lee University, and his theological training at Union Theological Seminary. Later Hampden-Sydney College conferred upon him the degree of D. D.

At the death of Dr. Theodorick Pryor, an uncle-in-law for whom he was named, Dr. Epes was called to minister to his own people in Nottoway from 1891 until the time of his death in 1911.

A beautiful bronze tablet to his memory by Frederick MacMonnies, the noted sculptor of New York and Paris, hangs upon the walls of the Presbyterian Church at Blackstone which Dr. Epes built during his pastorate here.

His son, Hon. Louis S. Epes, is now Justice of the Supreme Court of Virginia.

Miss Fannie Harris Epes, the only daughter of Thomas Freeman Epes, was a lady of unusual Christian character, and as a teacher in the little Fernhill School near her home exerted a marked influence on the children of the neighborhood.

The present owner of Windrow, Branch Bocock, has done much to restore the old house to its former state.

HIGH PEAK, not far from Windrow, was the home of John Segar Epes, a son of Thomas Freeman Epes and Jacqueline Hardaway Epes, of Windrow, who married Fannie Washington Epes. High Peak was named for High Peak in Prince George County, an estate not far from City Point belonging to Colonel Peter Epes, from whom Mrs.

John Segar Epes was descended. Mrs. John Segar Epes was a daughter of Francis Washington Epes and Susan Doswell, of Cedar Grove, in Nottoway. Francis Washington Epes was the son of Peter Epes and Rebecca Cross, who were married in 1798. This Peter Epes was the son of Colonel Peter Epes of High Peak, who married Mary Poythress. John Segar Epes served in the Nottoway Reserves during the Civil War.

THE OLD PLACE, situated on the road from the Poor House by Frank's Shop to Nottoway Court House, was the first settlement of the Epes family in Nottoway. The original house was built about 1760. Francis Epes of Causons in Prince George County patented the land here in 1735, four hundred acres. Francis Epes of Causons lived in the Parish of Martins Brandon in Prince George County. Causons was situated on the Appomattox River on the east side of Causon's Creek, near where the National Cemetery at Hopewell is now. This place should not be confused with Cawsons, the estate of Theodorick Bland an the west side of the creek. Francis Epes married Sarah Hamlin and was living at Causons as far back as 1722. This was a part of the original tract of 1700 acres granted to Captain Francis Epes August 26, 1635, for bringing over himself and three sons, John, Francis, and Thomas, and thirty other persons in 1629 and earier dates.

Francis Epes of Causons was the son of Wil-

WINDROW

Formerly the home of Thomas Freeman Epes, now owned by
Branch Bocock.

liam Epes who died prior to 1712. Circumstantial evidence would seem to show that this William Epes was the William Epes who was Sheriff of Prince George County in 1705, and that he was the son of Colonel John Epes, the eldest son of Francis Epes, the immigrant.

This Francis Epes of Causons did not move to Nottoway, nor did his son Colonel Peter Epes of High Peak in Prince George County.

However, another son, Colonel Francis Epes, Jr., came to Nottoway and settled on this four hundred acres deeded to him by his father in 1755. The place has always been known as the Old Place. Colonel Francis Epes, Jr., who died in 1789, married Mary Williams, daughter of Thomas Williams and Rachael Freeman. Rachael Freeman was a daughter of John Freeman, of Wellesley, Gloustershire, England.

In addition to this four hundred acres, Colonel Francis Epes, Jr., purchased fourteen hundred and fifty-two acres from Thomas Bowery of the island of Saint Christopher's in the British West Indies, which was a part of the twenty-seven hundred acres patented by his uncle, Isham Epes, a brother of Francis Epes, of Causons, both of whom were members of the House of Burgeses from Prince George County.

Colonel Francis Epes, Jr., was elected sergeant-at-arms of the Virginia House of Burgesses in 1752 and was sergeant-at-arms of the First House of Delegates in 1776, with his son, Colonel Freeman Epes, as deputy.

Colonel Freeman Epes was born about 1750 and married 1780 to Jane Wynn, daughter of John and Susanna Wynn. He lived on Lazaretta Creek, near Nottoway Court House, and was county lieutenant 1789-1800, and a member of the House of Delegates 1798-1800. His two daughters, Sarah, born March 23, 1793, and died November 26, 1833, and Martha, widow of Peter Branch Jones, were the first and second wives of Dr. Archibald Algernon Campbell, of Blendon, in Nottoway.

Major John Epes, a son of Colonel Francis Epes, Jr., next lived at the Old Place. He married twice. His first wife was Rachael Williams and his second, Frances Harris Campbell. After the death of Major John Epes, his widow lived here with her son, Thomas Freeman. Thomas Freeman Epes later moved to Windrow, which he purchased from Dr. Theodorick Pryor, whose wife was a sister of Thomas Freeman Epes. At the death of his mother, Thomas Freeman purchased the Old Place and later gave it to his son, James F. Epes, whose wife was Rebecca Poague, of Rockbridge County. The old house was burned by Federal soldiers in 1865 after the surrender. The present house was built by James F. Epes, who was the last Epes to live here. The place, now known as Broad Acre Farm, is owned by W. H. Moore.

Just before the Civil War, James F. Epes was a law student at the University of Virginia. Immediately upon the receipt of the news that Virginia had seceeded, he started home, and was met at Nottoway Court House by his father. He served throughout the war in Company E, 3rd Virginia Cavalry. During the course of the war he had two horses shot from under him, and was wounded at Reams Station just before the surrender. The war ended, he settled at the Old Place, after taking his law degree at Washington and Lee University. He served the county as Commonwealth's Attorney from 1870 to 1873.

The Fourth District owes an eternal debt of gratitude to James F. Epes, as it was through his efforts, assisted by Sidney P. Epes, Walter A. Watson and Captain J. M. Harris, that this district was rid of negro rule. In 1890 Mr. Epes reluctantly agreed to accept the nomination for Congress, a very thankless undertaking at that time, as the Fourth District was then represented by John M. Langston, a negro, who had just unseated Hon. E. C. Venable, of Petersburg. So well did Mr. Epes conduct his campaign, however, that he defeated Langston, and was again returned to Congress in 1892. He died August 24, 1910, in his 69th year.

OAKWOOD on the Cottage road near The Old Place is one of the prettiest homes in the county, a large brick house set in a beautiful grove of oaks. Freeman Epes, son of Thomas Freeman Epes, of Windrow, and brother of Hon. Jas. F. Epes, built the house after the war entirely from materials on the place, and here he brought his wife, Rebecca Robinson.

He was one of the most public spirited men of his generation, and gave unstintingly of his time and energy to the community. He was rightly called "the Father of Blackstone" on account of his untiring efforts to build up the town. He served in the Civil War in Company E, 3rd Virginia Cavalry.

ELMWOOD, not far from Oakwood, was built by George Cralle, who first married Sarah Mildred Carter. By this marriage there were the following children, G. Truly, who married Eliza Gilliam Willson of Amelia county, George A., Nannie, who married John Richard Hatchett of Lunenburg County, and Sarah, who married James Ferguson, of Dinwiddie. George Cralle later married Katherine Spottswood Bolling, a great niece of Thomas Jefferson. Their son, William Hatchett Cralle, who married Sallie Fletcher Hardaway, now lives at Elmwood. The Cralle family came to Nottoway from Northumberland County, and are of the French Huguenot descent. Richard Kenner Cralle, a relative of the Cralle family of Nottoway, was the intimate friend and biographer of John C. Calhoun.

UNION ACADEMY, a short distance west of Blackstone at the intersection of Cocke's and Brunswick roads, was once a school which flourished just before and soon after the war. This

ELMWOOD

Built by George Cralle, now the home of Willie Cralle

school was known as Union Academy and was run by Hardy and Crenshaw. Many boys came here from a distance as well as the boys in the neighborhood. So well was the school known that students came from the far South, and Dr. Hurt had to build a house to accommodate those who boarded at his home.

Dr. Walter Reed, who afterwards did so much for humanity in stamping out yellow fever, attended school here during the early years of the Civil War while his father, Rev. Lemuel S. Reed, was a pastor on this circuit.

AUBURN, a short distance down the Brunswick road, was the home of Dr. Jethro Meriwether Hurt, who married Virginia Irby, daughter of William Blunt Irby, of Pleasant Hill, in Nottoway. Dr. Hurt was the son of Meriwether Hurt and his second wife, Amy Morgan, a daughter of Captain Samuel Morgan, of Morgansville, in Nottoway. Two of his brothers, Josephus and Samuel, settled in Petersburg. Josephus married Arabella Smith, and Samuel married Elizabeth Stith, of Brunswick county. Another brother, Romulus, married Carrie Hardy, and lived in Nottoway at Maple Grove. His two sisters, Emily and Minerva, married brothers, Thomas and Phineas Fowlkes, respectively. Dr. Hurt was a prominent physician, and a man greatly beloved in the community. He was one of the organizers of the first agricultural club of Nottoway County, among whose members were Dr. Hurt, William Bland, William Blunt Irby, Captain Richard Irby, Dr. Campbell, Colonel Travis Epes, Thomas Freeman Epes, Dr. Blandy, and Dr. Sydnor. He was also one of the founders of St. Luke's Episcopal Church, and its Senior Warden for many years. He was educated at the University of Virginia and the Jefferson Medical College of Philadelphia. He was a member of Company G, the Nottoway Grays.

His son, Joseph Mettauer Hurt, did much for his county, and succeeded his father as Senior Warden of St. Luke's Church. He was at one time president of the Virginia Bankers Association, a member of the William and Mary Board for seven years, and a member of the legislature, sessions 1920-22-24. He died in Rochester, Minn., at the Mayo Hospital, December 4, 1925, age sixty-four years.

WOODLAND, built by Major John L. Morgan, who later sold it to John L. Irby, Sr., is near Auburn. John L. Irby, Sr., married Arianna Williams, daughter of David G. Williams. He did not live long and left the place to his son, John L. Irby, Jr., who married his cousin, Fannie Betty Irby. John L. Irby, Jr., served in the Civil War in Company E, 3rd Virginia Cavalry, but was detailed by General Fitzhugh Lee as his personal courier and scout.

Mr. Irby recalls the following incident. Just before the surrender at Appomattox, General Fitzhugh Lee had left some horses of his command in charge of his servant, and they had become separated from the regiment. Upon learning of this, John L. Irby, who was himself separated from his command on account of a sick horse, presented himself to General Robert E. Lee, and asked permission to take the horses and make his way to General Fitzhugh Lee, who he thought, was on his way south to join General Joseph E. Johnston.

General Lee, knowing the uselessness of such an attempt, said to him in his quiet way, "Sir, if you have come to me for such an order as this, I will have to order you to remain where you are". Mr. Irby said, "I will never forget the quiet dignified manner of General Lee, who must have been suffering agony because of the impending disaster, but whose countenance only reflected the consciousness of duty well done, and an abiding faith in a Divine Providence."

MAPLE GROVE, a few miles from Auburn, was built by a Mr. Buford of Brunswick County. Later it became the home of Romulus Hurt, who married Carrie Hardy. Rom. Hurt served in Company G, the 18th Virginia Regiment "The Nottoway Grays" during the War Between the States.

FALKLAND. Coming back towards Blackstone by what is known as the Ridge Road, we soon come to Falkland, where John G. Powell, who married Americus Wadell, lived.

SALLARDS, another old place on this road, was the home of Sam Scott, who married Miss Wilson, and later married the widow Goodwin. The widow Goodwin was a woman of means, and as she had several children by her first marriage, she insisted upon a marriage contract. Mr. Scott consented to this, but told her they would be married first and then go by the Court House and have the contract drawn up. To this she agreed. After the marriage they went to the Court House, and Mrs. Scott was told by the clerk that she was now Mrs. Sam Scott, and as such she had no right to insist upon a marriage contract. There is no evidence that they ever lived any less happily afterwards because of the lack of one.

Dr. John Fitzgerald's son, Jack Fitzgerald, married a daughter of Sam Scott. Dr. Fitzgerald's diploma from the University of Edinburgh, Scotland, was found a few years ago in the walls of this old house.

POPLAR HILL is about two and a half miles from Blackstone on Cocke's road. This place was called Batts when William Irby bought it from Richard Cross in 1792 for his son, Edmund. Edmund Irby built the present house in 1812. The bridge across the Little Nottoway River not far from the house was then called Batts' Bridge, while the one across Big Nottoway River, several miles away, was called Cross's bridge after the Richard Cross, who lived here.

POPLAR HILL

(Now called The Elms) built by Edmund Irby, 1812. Remodeled and enlarged by Captain Richard Irby, 1859.

Edmund Irby married Frances Briggs Lucas, of Greenville County, Virginia. He was a man of means, and a large slave owner. He also kept a goodly string of race horses, and his farm book, with a list of his slaves and race horses, is still extant, being in the hands of his granddaughter.

Edmund Irby was a great friend of John Randolph, of Roanoke, who once said of him that he was the best farmer in Virginia. He seemed to have gained the confidence and friendship of this brilliant but erratic statesman to a remarkable degree, and Mr. Randolph was a frequent visitor at Poplar Hill. He used to visit here to attend the races at Bellefonte and perhaps to break his journey to the Hermitage in Amelia on his way to see the only sweetheart he ever had, the beautiful Maria Ward. She afterwards discarded him to marry his cousin, Peyton Randolph, author of "The Reports of the Court of Appeals of Virginia." In Mr. Randolph's will may be seen the following entry: "I leave to Edmund Irby, of Nottoway, the next choice of my mares or fillies, and any one of my horses or colts to be selected by himself, also my double gun." Edmund Irby did not live to receive the bequest, however, as he died in 1829, four years before Mr. Randolph's death.

At Christmas, 1831, two years later, from Roanoke Mr. Randolph sent a Bible to the widow of Edmund Irby, and in it the following beautiful tribute to his friends at Poplar Hill was written on the fly leaf: "To the respected widow of my departed friend, Edmund Irby, of Nottoway, Esq. by one who entertains the sincerest esteem and regard for her character, and who will never cease but with life to feel the deepest interest in the family of a man who was honorably esteemed by all who knew him, and especially by those who were admitted to his confidence and friendship, of which honor the writer of these lines will ever cherish a mournful but proud recollection." At the death of Edmund Irby's widow, Poplar Hill passed to her son, Richard.

Richard Irby married Virginia Fitzgerald, of Leinster in Nottoway. He was living at Poplar Hill when the war broke out and at once enlisted in the Nottoway Grays, Company G. He was made first lieutenant of the company in 1861, and elected captain a year later of this intrepid band which was practically wiped out at the battle of Gettysburg in Pickett's immortal charge. At the battle of Second Manassas, Captain Irby was wounded twice.

At one time he served in the General Assembly of Virginia and was the author of "History of the Nottoway Grays", "History of Randolph-Macon College," "Bird Notes and Other Sketches." He was later Secretary and Treasurer of Randolph-Macon College.

He established a large foundry near his home, which he operated just before and for some time after the war. Poplar Hill was later sold by him to Charles Betts Hardy, who married Jane Clarkson Barnes. Charles Hardy served in Company G, 9th Virginia Cavalry, a Lunenburg Company commanded by Captain Stith Bolling. He changed the name of Poplar Hill to The Elms, which is the name of the place at the present time.

About a half mile from The Elms is the Little Nottoway River. In the old days, Batt's bridge crossed the river several hundred yards below where the present bridge is now, and there was an immense mill pond here, made by a dam near the forks of the Big and Little Nottoway rivers. Abraham Cocke operated the mill, and was granted in 1740 by the court a road to his mill. The road came to be known as Cocke's road or Cocke's lane. That is how this road received its name, and not, as some believe, from Dr. Cox, who perished in the big snow of 1857 which bears his name. The road was called Cocke's road as far back as 1740. John and Stephen Cocke, descendants of Abraham Cocke, were operating the mill in 1792.

DOBBINS is not far from the river on the left, and is an old settlement, a part of the Cocke plantation. Dr. John D. Blackwell taught a school here the last year of the war, and his son, Dr. R. E. Blackwell, now president of Randolph-Macon College, attended.

After the war, W. C. Irby, Sr., bought the place and named it Rural Oaks. Wesley Irby married first Mary William Jones, whose father owned Warren White Sulphur Springs in Warren

(35)

County, North Carolina, where General Lee's daughter, Annie, died in 1862 and is buried. He next married Margaret Barrett Hardaway, of Nottoway. His son, W. C. Irby, Jr., now lives at Rural Oaks.

HAZEL DELL is on the right and was, built by David G. Williams for his son, Fayette C. Williams, who married Anne Elizabeth Harrison, of North Carolina, January 7th, 1857. Their children were Margaret, who married John P. Irby; India, who married Henry Stokes; Dr. Fayette C., who married Ella Walker, of Tennessee; and Harrison L., who married Tera Walker, also of Tennessee. Fayette Williams was a lieutenant in Company E, 3rd Virginia Cavalry.

John P. Irby afterwards lived here, and still owns the plantation.

David G. Williams, who was a son of Thomas Roper Williams, of Nottoway, and who married Mary Epes Poythress Doswell, a daughter of Major John Doswell, of Cedar Grove, was immensely wealthy. He lived in Lunenburg County, but owned land all over Nottoway. He was said to have been the second largest slave owner in Virginia, having so many slaves that he did not know his own when he met them in the road. His father, Thomas Roper Williams, married Catherine Greenhill, a daughter of Colonel William C. Greenhill, of Greenhill, on Sellar Creek, who figured in the duel of Dr. Hardaway and Dr. Bacon. They had fourteen children, and nearly

HAZEL DELL

Built by David G. Williams for his son, Fayette C. Williams,
later the home of John P. Irby.

all of the fourteen had Greenhill for their middle name.

GLEN COVE is a short distance from Hazel Dell on the left, sitting well back from the road and surrounded by a beautiful fringe of old box. This was the home of Robert Scott, who married first Miss Hamlin, and second, Nov. 10, 1852, Mary Elizabeth Marshall. Their children were Petronella, who married Walter M. Irby; Fannie, who married James A. Walker; John, who married first, Sarah Guy, and second, Epes Shore, and A. Glenn, who married Florence Craig. J. A. Walker now lives here.

VERMONT. Leaving Cocke's road and turning to the right down what is known as the Stingy Lane road, we soon come to Vermont. This was the home of Captain Richard Jones, whose wife was Elizabeth Epes. Captain Jones was Commonwealth's Attorney of Nottoway and a veteran of the War of 1812. He was the owner of the Bellefonte race track and moved from Vermont in 1839 to Bellefonte, where he made his home until his death. Thomas Williams, who married Kate Redd, lived here after the war.

ROVER'S REST is an old home in this neighborhood a few miles from Vermont, whose chimneys and foundations, cut from solid rock in immense squares, must have required months to build. Joel Williams, who married Helen Smith, October

31, 1855, lived here, as did Dr. Joseph Addison Jones, who married Mary Frances Irby.

In the western part of Nottoway, which borders on Prince Edward and Lunenburg Counties, were some of the finest homes in antebellum days. Here lived the Carter, Fowlkes, Oliver, Knight and Jeffress families.

OAKLAND was built in 1827 by Colonel Edward T. Jeffress, son of John Jeffress, who came to Nottoway from Lunenburg. He married twice; his first wife was Dicey Hall Fowlkes, sister of Paschal Fowlkes, of Hyde Park, and his second, Miss Gravatt of Caroline County. He was a large slave owner and for years conducted a mercantile business at Jeffress Store.

After Colonel Edward Jeffress died, his son, Luther Jeffress, who married Elizabeth Wilson, lived at Oakland. After his death, his son, William Horace Jeffress, who married Victoria H. Wilson, of Baltimore, inherited the property and was the last Jeffress to live here. Horace Jeffress served in the Confederate Army, first in a Nottoway and then in a Charlotte Company. He was wounded at the battle of Williamsburg, and from the effect of this wound he never recovered, always walking with a limp. Oakland has recently burned. The boxwood which surrounded the front yard was very beautiful, and was sold after the fire by the present owner for eighteen hundred dollars.

WOODVILLE, another Jeffress home not far away, was the home of Colonel William Calvin Jeffress, who bought the place in 1847. Colonel Jeffress married three times. His first wife was a Miss Clarke. One child by this marriage, Robert Alexander, moved to Texas and died there. His second wife, Miss Mosley, had the following children: Howard, Edward T., and Margaret. His third wife, Miss Thornton, had three children: Thornton, Walter C., and Sallie F. Colonel Calvin Jeffress was the commanding officer of Jeffress Battery, the Nottoway Artillery Company, and served with distinction throughout the war. He afterwards sold Woodville and bought Mountain Hall.

HYDE PARK, not far from Oakland, was the home of Paschal Fowlkes, who married Martha Hyde. This is one of the handsomest homes in the county. It is of a very unusual construction in that it is part frame and part brick. The original part of the house built by Paschal Fowlkes is frame. The grounds and lawn are very beautiful with immense trees and formal gardens. Dr. Frank Fowlkes, who married his cousin, Lucy Fowlkes, later lived here. The property afterwards passed to a Northern man, a Mr. Scott, who greatly enlarged the house, which consists now of twenty-five rooms, one of which is an immense ball room.

INWOOD, a short distance from Hyde Park, the home of Colonel W. C. Knight, a son of Colonel John H. Knight, was built by him in 1842-43. Colonel W. C. Knight was one of the outstanding men in the community, often serving as chairman of the different political meetings held in the county. He was a member of the State Senate and afterwards owner and editor of the Southern Planter, and president of the Virginia State Agricultural Society.

Colonel Knight was twice married. His first wife was Bettie Garrant Dickinson of Inverness in Nottoway, and his second, Miss Thomas, of Richmond. In 1858 Colonel Knight sold Inwood and bought Wilton, the old Randolph estate on the James River. Former Lieutenant Governor J. Taylor Ellyson's father owned Inwood at the outbreak of the war. The grounds at Inwood in those days were very beautiful, laid out with fountains and formal gardens. In later years it was known as the Stearn's place.

CLEARMONT was the home of Colonel John Hughes Knight, whose wife was Sallie Carter. He was the father of Colonel W. C. Knight, Captain John Hughes Knight, and Dr. Oscar M. Knight. Clearmont was a few miles from Inwood. Colonel John Hughes Knight was a member of the legislature, and was on the Corresponding Committee to instruct for Andrew Jackson for President from Nottoway County.

His son, Dr. Oscar M. Knight, who married

HYDE PARK

The home of Paschal Fowlkes, later the home of
Dr. Frank Fowlkes

Ellen Todd, later lived here. Dr. Knight at the time of his death was the oldest alumnus of Virginia Military Institute, being a member of the first graduating class turned out by that institution.

Colonel John H. Knight's son, Captain John H. Knight, moved to Prince Edward County and lived at Poplar Hill near Farmville. His son, John Thornton Knight, was a brilliant officer in the United States Army, rising to the rank of Brigadier General. An account of his record is given in the Hampden-Sydney magazine and is as follows:

"John Thornton Knight, 1880, Brigadier General, U. S. A., retired, died at his home in San Francisco, California, after a brief illness of pneumonia, January 15, 1930. He was the son of the late Captain John H. Knight of Poplar Hill, Prince Edward County, Virginia, and was born April 18, 1861.

"He received his preparatory training at Prince Edward Academy, Worsham, Virginia, under Professor James R. Thornton and entered Hampden-Sydney College in 1877, a member of the class of 1880. In 1879 he entered the U. S. Military Academy at West Point and in due time graduated (1884) and received a commission as second lieutenant of cavalry in the U. S. Army.

"After service in the West, he was appointed Commandant of Cadets at the Virginia Polytechnic Institute; then fought in Cuba during the Spanish-American War; and for some years was stationed in the Philippine Islands where he rendered valuable service, as also in China and Japan.

"In the World War his work was especially noteworthy. He was Quarter-Master of the Port of Embarkation, Newport News, Virginia, August, 1917, to September, 1918; served overseas at Quarter-Masters Base, Brest, France, October, 1918, to January, 1919; was Chief Quarter-Master, A. E. F., April to September, 1919, with supervision extending to England, Belgium, Germany, Luxemburg, Spain, Italy, and Russia. He was made Commander of the Order of Leopold—a citation conferred by the King of Belgium and was commended by President Wilson for specially meritorious work as Quarter-Master at Newport News, Virginia.

"This military record, one of distinguished service, speaks for itself; but it does not give the intimate picture of the man as his friends knew him. Physically, no one could have looked the soldier more completely—six feet and more in height, erect, and strikingly handsome. As stated above, General Knight's first commission was in the cavalry. This was due in large measure to his superb horsemanship. There are those yet living who remember his skill and grace in the cavalry drills on the old parade grounds at the Military Academy. Some one has said that Virginians made such splendid soldiers in the War Between the States because they ride, shoot, and tell the truth. General Knight excelled in all three of these qualifications. His magnificent seat in the saddle reminded one of those great Virginia Cavalrymen—Stuart and Fitz Lee.

"At the same time, his was one of the most lovable of natures—kindly, sweet-tempered, generous, loyal. He was a man with whom one liked to associate—affectionate but sincere, firm but kind, conscientious but tolerant—the embodiment of that rare and charming trait, manly gentleness.

"Since his retirement, General Knight had made his home in San Francisco, and was buried at the Presidio there with the usual military honors. He is survived by his widow, four sons, and a daughter. Three sisters still reside in Prince Edward—Miss Bettie B. Knight and Mrs. W. G. Dunnington of Poplar Hill, and Mrs. J. B. Strachan, of Farmville."

PLENTIFUL LEVEL is in this neighborhood, the home of the Carters. Three generations of Carters have lived here. Raleigh Carter, who married Sarah Sharpe, was the first. He was Colonial Justice of Amelia County in 1782 and Sheriff of Nottoway 1792. His son, Charles Carter, who married Miss Coleman, was the next and Wesley Carter, who married his cousin, Nannie Carter, was the last of the Carters to live here.

HICKORY HILL was the home of Sharpe Carter, who married Martha Gregory and is a short distance from Plentiful Level. Major Leroy Long, whose wife was Ada Hutter, afterwards lived here, and named the place Carter's Hall. He was a major in the Confederate Army and served on General Longstreet's Staff. His brother, General Armstead L. Long, was Military Secretary to General Robert E. Lee and Chief of Artillery, 2nd Corps, Army Northern Virginia, and was also the author of "Memoirs of Robert E. Lee." Colonel William R. Carter, a son of Sharpe Carter, was colonel of 3rd Virginia Cavalry and died in Richmond of fever during the Civil War. Colonel William R. Carter and Major Leroy Long are both buried at Carter's Hall.

WOODLAND on Nottoway River was built in 1807 by Kenner Cralle, born 1774, whose wife was Nancy Hatchett. Kenner Cralle was the father of George A. Cralle of Elmwood, and of Grief Cralle, who never married. Grief Cralle inherited Woodland and lived there until his death. He was a man of forceful character. It is interesting to note that he once changed the course of Nottoway River bordering on his plantation. Major Leroy Long once lived here and later moved to Hickory Hill.

OAK GROVE, so called because the house is set in a beautiful grove of oaks, is near Plentiful Level and was the home of John B. Oliver, who married Jane Carter, a sister of Sharpe Carter. This place was sometimes called "Fritter Grove," because it was said that fritters were nearly al-

INWOOD

Built by Colonel W. C. Knight in 1842-43, later known as
the Stearn's place.

ways served here for desert. It was also called Fair View. John B. Oliver's children were Lucy Jane, who married Dr. R. B. Tuggle, of Raven-wood, and Charles H.., who married Miss Ingram from Missouri.

HERA, built by William Farmer, near Oak Grove, was once a Scott settlement. In late years it was owned by Henry Lee, who married Helen Fitzgerald.

ROSELAND, built in June 1811 by Elisha Dickinson, is on Big Nottoway River and joins Inwood. It was the home of Colonel William Purnell Dickinson, born Sept. 7, 1810, died October 6, 1874, who married first Miss Barksdale of Charlotte County, Virginia, and later Miss Venable of Prince Edward County, by whom he had two daughters. Still later he married Miss Rosamond Smith, of Lunenburg County, born June 20, 1833, died September 3, 1896, and by this union there were eight children. Their son, William Dupuy Dickinson, who married Miss Mary Johns, of Texas, now owns Roseland and lives there.

CEDAR GROVE, near the Falls of Nottoway, was built by Major John Doswell, whose wife was Mary Poythress Epes, daughter of Colonel Peter Epes of High Peak in Prince George County, who was a brother of Colonel Francis Epes, Jr., of "The Old Place."

Major Doswell was Justice of Nottoway in 1793, and later Sheriff. His son, John Doswell, inherited the plantation, but died as a young man, and the property then passed to Major Doswell's daughter, Frances Susan Doswell, who married twice; first Harry Stanard Beverley, and after his death, Francis Washington Epes, a son of Peter Epes and Rebecca Cross, and grandson of Colonel Peter Epes, of High Peak in Prince George County. Washington Epes and Susan Beverley, nee Doswell, were married September 10, 1839, and lived at Cedar Grove for a number of years. Major Doswell's daughters all married prominent men. Mary Epes Poythress Doswell married David G. Williams; Sallie Epes Doswell married Henry Cabell; and Martha Doswell married Colins Buckner.

Major John Doswell and Francis Washington Epes with their wives are buried at Cedar Grove.

ASPEN CIRCLE is not far from Cedar Grove. This was the home of Benjamin Fitzgerald, who married Elizabeth Ward. He was the son of Francis Fitzgerald of The Castle. Dr. Joseph A. Jones at one time lived here also. It is now known as the Old Burton Place.

PEA RIDGE, a quarter settlement, which belonged to Benjamin Fitzgerald, and **Mulberry Grove,** an Oliver home, are both in this neighborhood.

CHESTNUT HILL is on the road between the Falls of Nottoway and Crewe, and was the home of Liberty Fowlkes, a veteran of the Civil War, for a number of years. He married twice; his first wife was Harriett Bruce, and his second, Sallie Ellington. His son, Truly Fowlkes, who married first Miss Burton, and second Miss Marshall, now lives here.

EDGE HILL is on this road too, the old Ingram home. In ante-bellum days, Stith Ingram lived here, and afterwards it was the home of his son, Dick Ingram, who married Miss Boxley, of Kentucky. Dick Ingram served in the Civil War in Company E, 3rd Virginia Cavalry, and his son, Macon Ingram now lives at Edge Hill.

MILLBROOK is a few miles from Edge Hill. In the old days it was the home of John D. Williams, a son of David G. Williams, whose wife was Martha Bland. Their daughter, Mary Elizabeth Poythress Williams, married Samuel Epes, of Battle View. Later Henry Fowlkes, who married Miss Ingram, lived here. The home is now owned by Virginius Fowlkes.

OAKRIDGE, on the Hungary Town road, which in old times was called Jordan's road, was built about 1800, and was first the seat of the Smiths and later the home of the Guys.

Captain Warner Wortham Guy, who married Hannah Scott January 3, 1822, came to Nottoway in 1842, after his wife's death. He later married Mrs. Mary Smith, nee Winn, September 8, 1842, and settled at Oakridge, where he lived until his death in 1863. His son, Colonel William Scott Guy, a son by his first marriage, next lived here. Colonel William Scott Guy, a graduate of Virginia Military Institute, served with distinction during the Civil War. At the outbreak of the war, he was teaching school in North Carolina. He at once organized a company, the Granville Grays, and shortly afterwards was elected lieutenant colonel of a North Carolina regiment. His health broke down, however, and he was forced to come home. After recovering his health, he joined the Nottoway Cavalry and served until the end of the war. When General Lee surrendered, Colonel Guy started to North Carolina to join General Joseph E. Johnston, but learning of General Johnston's surrender, he returned home and was paroled at Nottoway Court House. Colonel Guy was wounded twice during the course of the war, eventually losing the sight of one eye from the effect of a wound. Colonel William Scott Guy married July 24, 1883, Elizabeth Bouldin Williams, a daughter of Thomas W. and Katherine Redd Williams, of Vermont, in Nottoway. His brother, Francis Wortham Guy, left Emory and Henry College in 1861 to join the Nottoway Cavalry and was killed at Atlee Station, May 28, 1864.

Oakridge has some beautiful mantels and paneling, and a very unique stairway, built after the order of Chinese Chippendale. There is a Smith grave in the old garden at the rear of the house with large marble slabs. These slabs were removed during the war by a Yankee soldier looking for silver ware, and have never been replaced. John B. Tuggle, who married Lucy Mason, lived here for a while after the war. In later years, Mr. Stockton, a Northern man, bought the place, and has done much to restore it to its former beauty. The original estate comprised about 4,000 acres.

WHETSTONE, a few miles from Oakridge, was the home of Dr. Joseph Addison Jones, who married Mary Frances Irby, June 18, 1856. John Ingram, who married first the widow Hawkins and later Miss Weileman, both of Mississippi, afterwards lived here.

JORDANS was a quarter settlement owned by Dr. John Shore and is located on this road.

RIVER VIEW, not far from Jordans, was a part of the old Edmund Irby tract and owned by Frank White, who married first Haynie Hardy, and second Nannie Smith, both of Lunenburg County. Frank White served in Company G, 9th Virginia Cavalry, a Lunenburg Company under command of Captain Stith Bolling during the Civil War. His son, Frank, now lives here.

PLEASANT HILL. Crossing the Little Nottoway over what used to be called Jordan's bridge, to the left is Pleasant Hill. This was the first Irby settlement in Nottoway. Charles Irby, the first of the Irbys to settle in Nottoway, came from Prince George County in 1733 and settled on four hundred acres of land left him by his father, Edmund Irby, of Prince George. Later he patented seven hundred and sixty acres on the north side of Little Nottoway River. He was a Colonial Justice of Amelia in 1735 and later Sheriff. It is not known definitely where his home was located.

In 1780 his nephew, William Irby, moved to Nottoway from Sussex County and built the house at Pleasant Hill. William Irby was married twice; first to Jane Edmunds, and later to Elizabeth Williams, daughter of Thomas Roper Williams, of Nottoway.

His son by the second marriage, William Blunt Irby, next lived here, whose wife was Sarah Washington Stith, daughter of Major John Stith, a soldier of the Revolutionary War, who served on General Lafayette's Staff. She was a granddaughter of Lawrence Washington, of Chotank, King George County, Virginia.

They had ten children, five sons, John, Freeman, Edward, George and Walter, and five daughters, Elizabeth Anne, Sarah, Virginia, Mary Frances and Minerva.

Two of the sons, John and Edward, were physicians and went south to practice their profession. Three daughters also married physicians, Virginia marrying Dr. J. M. Hurt, Mary Frances, Dr. Joseph A. Jones, and Sarah, Dr. Richard Burke. Dr. Burke and his wife lived at Pleasant Hill with her parents, while he practiced his profession in the county. It may be of interest to the people of Nottoway that in January, 1852, Dr. Burke wrote to his brother-in-law, Dr. John W. Irby in Mississippi. "The Southside Railroad which you know is to be run from Petersburg to Lynchburg is getting on very well and is now in full operation from Blacks and Whites to Petersburg, and will be by the first of February completed to Nottoway Court House."

William Blunt Irby was sixty-one years of age when the Civil War came on. Although too old to go himself, his sons, Edward, George and Walter, early enlisted in the army and a grandson, his namesake, was killed at Murfreesboro, Tennessee.

Walter and George Irby served in Company E, Nottoway Cavalry, while Edward was captain of a Tennesse Company and was severely wounded at Belmont, Missouri. Another son, Freeman Buckner Irby, served with credit in the Mississippi Legislature at its most critical period.

William Blunt Irby died in 1896 at Auburn, the home of his daughter, Mrs. Virginia Hurt, in his ninety-seventh year, having lived during the life of every President of the United States from Washington to Cleveland. It is a remarkable fact, and shows how young our country is, that people now living should have seen and talked to a man, who lived during the lifetime of General Washington. W. B. Irby, the present owner of the plantation, is a direct descendant of William Irby, who built the house in 1780. The original house, however, has been replaced by one of later design.

THE BOWERY is on this road too.

The land here was originally patented by Isham Epes, of Bath Parish, Prince George County, in 1734 and 1745, a tract of twenty-seven hundred acres. Isham Epes was a brother of Francis Epes of Causons in Prince George County, and, like his brother, did not move to Nottoway. Isham Epes afterwards, in 1745, sold to Thomas Bowery of the island of Saint Christopher's in the British West Indies nineteen hundred and ninety-three acres; hence, the name of the place, "The Bowery".

Later Colonel Francis Epes, Jr., a nephew of Isham Epes and son of Francis Epes, of Causons, purchased from Thomas Bowery fourteen hundred and fifty-two acres, and his son, Captain Thomas Epes, inherited the property and settled at Poplar Hill. Near the site of his old home is now the home of Archer Epes. Captain Epes had a son, John Freeman Epes, who settled and probably built the present house at The Bowery. John Freeman Epes married Mary Anne Scott, a daughter of Sam Scott.

PLEASANT HILL

Built by William Irby of Sussex, 1780, later the home of
his son, William Blunt Irby.

Samuel Epes, a son of John Freeman Epes, next lived here. He married first Mary Elizabeth Poythress Williams, and second, the widow Maben. His first wife did not like the name "The Bowery" and changed the name of the place to Battle View on account of the nearness to the Grove battlefield.

This is a typical old house of the square colonial type, and has some beautiful wainscoating and mantels. The doors are very massive, with immense brass locks twelve by seven inches, and are made up of six panels with built-in crosses, which were said to be a protection against evil spirits. What was once a formal garden, with the largest box bushes in the county, is in the rear of the house.

Like most old homes, it has its ghost. A beautiful lady in bridal attire may be seen at twelve o'clock almost any moonlight night, as she appears on the north porch, and slowly descends the steps, crossing the yard and vanishing at the well.

H. B. Epes, a son of Samuel Epes, married Bena Haskins and now lives here.

WALNUT HILL is a short distance west of Blackstone on the Nottoway Court House road, the home first of the Epes family and later of the Fitzgeralds. This was a part of the land patented by Isham Epes in 1734 and 1745, and was settled by Colonel Richard Epes, a son of

Colonel Peter Epes and Mary Poythress Epes of High Peak in Prince George County.

Colonel Peter Epes of High Peak was a member of the Prince George Committee of Safety, 1775, and Sheriff in 1779. He was a brother of Colonel Francis Epes, Jr., and a son of Francis Epes of Causons. Colonel Richard Epes, who married Martha Greenhill Williams, a daughter of Thomas Roper Williams of Nottoway, was Sheriff of Nottoway in 1824. His son, Peter Epes, who married Martha C. Oliver, April 7, 1821, next lived at Walnut Hill. Their children were, Richard, who married Agnes Batte; Isaac O., who married Rosalie Beverley; Andrew J., who died a bachelor; Helen, who married Dr. Wm. J. Harris, and Matilda, who married William Bland. It was later the home of Jack Fitzgerald, a son of Dr. John Fitzgerald, who married Martha Scott, a daughter of Sam Scott of Sallards.

Mary Jane Anderson, the mother of the poet, Sidney Lanier, often visited at Walnut Hill when a young girl. After the war, John McEnery, who married Hannah Gilliam, lived at Walnut Hill for a long time. The place is now owned by B. R. Morse.

POPLAR HILL is across the road from Walnut Hill, built by Captain Thomas Epes and a part of the land originally patented by Isham Epes. Captain Thomas Epes was married twice; his first wife was Catherine Williams, and his second, Frances Scott, the widow of Archer Jones. His son, Richard Epes, the only child by his second marriage, who was known as Long Dick to distinguish him from Clerk Dick Epes, next lived here. His wife was Fannie Dunn. Archer Epes, a son of Richard Epes and Fannie Dunn Epes, now owns the place and makes it his home.

THE GROVE, a short distance farther on the Court House road to the left, was built on the site of The Grove battlefield by Richard Hardaway, who married Sallie Jones. Wilfred Tuggle, a son of Dr. R. B. Tuggle and Lucy Jane Oliver of Ravenswood in Nottoway, who married Clara Vass, later bought The Grove and lived there for a number of years. He was a man of quiet disposition, and took no active part in politics. A gentleman of the "old school", he fully lived up to what that term implies. His home was among the most hospitable in the county, and was always filled with guests. He served in the war in Company E, 3rd Virginia Cavalry.

CEDAR HILL is a mile or two back of The Grove, built by Stith Hardaway, who died a bachelor, and left the place to his nephew, Dr. Daniel Hardaway, a brother of Dr. John S. Hardaway, killed in the duel with Dr. Geo. S. G. Bacon at Nottoway Court House in 1818. Dr. Daniel Hardaway married Sallie Jones, and at his death left Cedar Hill to his son, Horace Hardaway, who married his cousin, Sallie Anne Hardaway. Horace Hardaway's son, Harvie, who married Sue Epes, lived here after the war.

Just after the battle of The Grove, Cedar Hill was used as a Federal hospital, and blood stains may still be seen on the floors, despite the efforts of later occupants to remove them.

In the raid of Kautz and Wilson, which later terminated in the battle of The Grove, Cedar Hill fared badly at the hands of the Federal troops, giving as the excuse for their vandalism that two members of the family were in the Confederate service. The raiders broke up most of the furniture, drove off the slaves, and took everything of value they could carry away with them. Daniel and Jack Hardaway, sons of Horace Hardaway, served in Company E, 3rd Virginia Cavalry.

LEINSTER on the Court House road a few miles from The Grove to the right was one of the first Fitzgerald settlements in Nottoway.

The house was built by Captain William Fitzgerald, II, who patented the land in 1742. He was the son of William Fitzgerald I, who came over from Ireland and settled in Prince George County. At the outbreak of the Revolutionary War, William Fitzgerald II, who married Sarah Epes, a sister of Major John Epes, was living at Leinster. He at once organized a company, was elected captain and served throughout the war. He was wounded at the battle of Guilford Court House, and was breveted major for gallantry in

WALNUT HILL

The home first of the Epes family and later of the Fitzgeralds.

action during that battle. Soon after the Revolutionary War, his first wife died, and he married a widow, Catherine Cralle Jones, who before her marriage was first the widow Ward, and then the widow Jones. She it was who was known as Catherine Cralle, "The Queen", having been quite a belle in her young days, marrying all three of her former suitors in turn: first, Colonel Benjamin Ward of West Creek; second, Daniel Jones of Mount Airy; and third, Colonel William Fitzgerald of Leinster. Her last marriage took place at Leinster, where her son, Benjamin Ward, Jr., and Captain William Fitzgerald's daughter, Sarah, were also married at the same time.

In later years, Mrs. Fitzgerald said that she regretted that she had gone to Leinster to be married, instead of having Captain Fitzgerald come to her home for the ceremony.

Dr. John Fitzgerald, a son of Captain William Fitzgerald, later lived at Leinster. Dr. Fitzgerald married Louisa Jones. He was a prominent physician in the county, and highly educated, having received his degree from the University of Edinburgh in Scotland. Freeman Fitzgerald, who married Elizabeth Williams Irby, later lived here. And still later it was the home of William Fitzgerald III, who married Sallie Anne Hardaway.

THE CASTLE, another Fitzgerald settlement, is located a short distance from Leinster on the opposite side of the road. Its name was first

Munster Castle, and was settled by Francis Fitzgerald, a brother of William Fitzgerald of Leinster. Francis Fitzgerald was in 1798 one of the early justices in the county. He married twice; his first wife was Mary Epes, a sister of the first Mrs. Fitzgerald of Leinster, and also a sister of Major John Epes. His second wife was Kate Ward. His daughter, Fannie, by this marriage, married Dr. Theodorick Pryor, much beloved Presbyterian minister who succeeded Dr. William S. White in Nottoway. Dr. Pryor built the Presbyterian Brick Church at Nottoway Court House in 1837. He died in 1890, and with his wife, Fannie Fitzgerald Pryor, is buried under the pulpit of this old church.

Francis Fitzgerald left The Castle to his two daughters, Fannie and Mary. Miss Mary Fitzgerald never married. Edwin Epes, a son of Colonel Travis Epes of Fancy Hill, who married Nannie Fitzgerald, lived here in later years. Edwin Epes was a member of Company E, 3rd Virginia Cavalry. His wife, Nannie Epes, nee Fitzgerald, was a daughter of William Fitzgerald, III, of Leinster, and granddaughter of Captain William Fitzgerald of the Revolutionary War.

With Mrs. Edwin Epes lived her sister, Miss Sallie Fitzgerald, a lady of forceful character and marked ability as a teacher and trainer of young people, who spent nearly her entire life teaching in the county.

The Castle, as well as Leinster have both been destroyed by fire.

ROSE HILL was about half way between Leinster and The Castle. This was the Presbyterian Manse, and the home of Dr. Theodorick Pryor, much beloved, who served the people of Nottoway County for nearly fifty years. He was married three times. His first wife was Lucy Atkinson, of Oliver Hill, in Chesterfield County; his second, Frances Epes, a sister of Thomas Freeman Epes of Nottoway; and his third, Fannie Fitzgerald of The Castle.

He was educated at Hampden-Sydney and studied law at the University of Virginia. After his first marriage, he practiced law for two years, but afterwards decided to enter the ministry, and began his pastorate in Nottoway in 1832.

Dr. Pryor's son, Roger Atkinson Pryor, by his first wife, was perhaps the most brilliant man who ever lived in Nottoway County. He was educated at Hampden-Sydney College and at the University of Virginia.

At one time he was editor of the Richmond Enquirer, was once Minister to Greece, a member of the old Congress and later a member of the Confederate Congress, and a brigadier general in the Confederate Army. Roger Pryor was an ardent secessionist, and it was due to his influence perhaps as much as to any one man that the War Between the States was precipitated.

He had tried in vain to get Virginia to secede. Failing in this, he left Virginia and went to South Carolina. Here he did his utmost in behalf of secession. In a speech at Charleston, South Carolina, April 10, 1861, he told his hearers that only one thing was necessary to force Virginia out of the Union—"A blow struck". "That done," he said, "Virginia will go out in less than one hour by Shrewsbury Clock". "The very moment," he declared, "that blood is shed, Old Virginia will make common cause with her sisters of the South." He was one of the four aides of General Beauregard who ordered the bombardment, and was accorded the honor of firing the first shot on Fort Sumter, but declined in favor of his friend, Edmund Ruffin, another Virginian, who is said to have fired the gun which started the conflict.

General Pryor became dissatisfied with his command, resigned, and joined Company E, the Nottoway Cavalry, as a private, and was later captured. After the war, with his fortune gone, Roger Pryor, with his wife, seven children, and three hundred dollars, borrowed upon a watch and a diamond ring, sought New York in order to retrieve his fortune, and began the practice of law. He became one of the leading lawyers among the brilliant coterie of lawyers of that city. Later made judge of the Court of Common Pleas, he retired from the bench in 1899.

He married Sarah Agnes Rice of Halifax County, Virginia, who matched her husband in brilliance. She was the author of "Reminiscences of Peace and War," and "My Day".

POPLAR HILL

Built by Captain Thomas Epes—His son, Richard Epes
(Long Dick) later lived here, now the home of Archer Epes.

TIP TOP, just east of the Court House, was the home of Richard Epes, who married Agnes Batte. Richard Epes, who was clerk of the county for twenty-eight years, was known as Clerk Dick to distinguish him from Richard Epes of Poplar Hill.

After the war Southern office holders were disfranchised, and he could not hold office until disabilities were removed. Then his friend, George Henry Southall, of Nottoway Court House, got the appointment as clerk and turned the office over to Mr. Epes. Later Richard Epes was again elected clerk of Nottoway County. He spent time and patience in having the mutilated records washed, cleaned, and pasted to book covers and files.

His son, Sidney P. Epes, who married Lucy Jones, daughter of Captain A. B. Jones, did much for his people and the Fourth District. Born August 20, 1865, a great part of his life was spent during the Reconstruction period, and much of his time and energy were given in the effort to better conditions which existed during that time. He was educated in Kentucky, and was for some time a newspaper editor.

He served in the House of Delegates, session 1891-92, and was later register of the land office of Virginia from 1895 until he was elected to the fifty-fifth Congress, but was later unseated by his Republican opponent. Undaunted, he again ran and was elected to the fifty-sixth Congress, dying March 3, 1900 while a member of that body.

EDGE HILL, situated back of the present Norfolk and Western Depot at Nottoway Court House, was once the home of Dr. John Patterson, and later, after the war, of Colonel Richmond F. Dillard. Colonel Dillard came to Nottoway from Sussex County. He married Martha Jane Massenburg of Greensville County. He was a member of the State Senate during the War Between the States, and at one time was a colonel in the Sussex County Militia. He operated a large hotel at Nottoway Court House after the war. He was buried at Edge Hill, but his remains were later moved to Blackstone.

NOTTOWAY COURT HOUSE is described in Martin's Gazetteer of Virginia about 1835, as follows:

"(Post-Village) sixty-seven miles west of Richmond and one hundred eighty-nine miles from Washington; situated on Nottoway River one mile east of Hendersonville in the business part of the county. It contains a Court House, Clerk's Office and criminal and debtor's jail, besides fifteen dwelling houses, one mercantile house, one hotel, one saddler, one tailor and one blacksmith shop. In the vicinity, on Nottoway River, there is a manufacturing flour mill. a daily stage passes this place on its route from Petersburg to North Carolina. Population seventy persons, of whom one is an attorney and one a regular physician." It was the scene of many court days, political meetings and stirring events. Here took place in 1847 the debate between George C. Droomgoole and Colonel George E. Bolling in the race for Congress, in which "Old Drum" so completely floored his opponent.

Here in 1860 Roger A. Pryor made the best speech of his career for Breckenridge.

On April 7, 1861, took place that memorable meeting, called to decide on secession. The sentiment was overwhelmingly for secession, Colonel Travis Epes of Fancy Hill standing almost alone against such a move. Colonel Epes, who always wore a tall beaver hat and Prince Albert coat, was a striking figure as he arose to address the meeting. Said Colonel Epes: "You do not know what you are doing in voting for secession. You cannot compete with the Federal Government; they will send an army here, despoil your homes, and free your slaves. Every able-bodied man before me will have to go into the army and try to repel the invaders. I have five sons who will have to go. Should Virginia secede, I will give everything I possess to her cause, but I am opposed to secession." He was howled down in derision and his brother, Thomas Freeman Epes, took him severely to task for his speech.

Old Dr. Campbell spoke, a venerable man with long gray hair. He made a ringing speech for secession in which he said: "I am too old to go into the army myself, but I will take old Ben (his carriage driver) and get in my carriage, and go up there, and shoot them through the windows." His speech was received with loud applause, and the meeting broke up with the delegates unanimously instructed for secession.

Virginia seceded on the 17th day of April, 1861. Immediately the men in the county were called to the colors, and Company E. Nottoway Cavalry was mobilized at Nottoway Court House.

The ladies in the county at once began to make a flag for them, and Miss Fannie Bettie Epes, a daughter of Colonel Travis Epes, gave a beautiful dark blue silk dress for the purpose. The ample cut in the style of the dresses of that day furnished abundant material. When the flag was ready, a large crowd assembled to witness the presentation ceremony. A big dinner was served on the court green. Reverend Edward M. Martin, pastor of the Presbyterian Church at Nottoway, offered a beautiful prayer and Hon. Thomas Campbell made the presentation speech. The company standing at attention to receive the colors, presented an inspiring spectacle. Hamlin Epes, the color-bearer, received the flag amid wild enthusiasm.

On April 21st, 1861, came the call from Governor Letcher to report to Richmond.

The company spent the first night in Amelia. Arriving in Richmond they were ordered to report to General J. B. Magruder at Yorktown. They took part in the battle of Big Bethel, the

CEDAR HILL

Built by Stith Hardaway, now the home of
Waverly Hammock.

first battle of the war, and served continuously until the end at Appomattox.

In the battle of Chancellorsville they fought with such conspicuous gallantry, that General Stuart himself complimented them highly for their valor.

On April 5, 1865, four years later almost to the day, General Grant occupied Nottoway Court House in pursuit of General Lee's Army, and received word here that General Sheridan was at Jetersville, across General Lee's line of retreat.

The Yankees used the pews in the Presbyterian Church for horse stalls, and ransacked the Clerk's Office, cutting the indexes out of the books and hacking them to pieces with their sabres, finally throwing them into the horse trough, where they were later rescued and returned to the Clerk's Office. In one of these old books may still be seen written by a Yankee soldier, "Abraham Lincoln, President of Virginia 1865."

It is unfortunate that these old books are still in the same condition in which they were left by General Grant's troops, when for a small outlay they could be put back in fair condition and re-indexed.

RAVENWOOD, just south of Nottoway Court House, was the home of Dr. R. B. Tuggle, who married Lucy Jane Oliver. Their children were Lacy, who married Judge Charles F. Goodwyn and lived at Worthams near the Court House;

Richard Wilfred, who married Clara Vass, and lived at The Grove; John B. who married Lucy Mason, of Petersburg; India, who married Samuel Davies, and Cammie, who married Robert Thornton, of Richmond.

Here are some beautiful stone steps, and also an ice house built entirely of stone, the work of Charles Hingston, an English stone mason, who lived in Nottoway before the war. Charles Hingston, an artist in his line, also built the chimneys and foundation at Rovers Rest, and the stone wall around the grave yard at Mountain Hall. At Dr. Tuggle's death, his widow was left very well off, and was considered so wealthy that in describing the wealth of others in the county, people would say, "He is as rich as Mrs. Lucy Jane Tuggle," or to spend that much money "would break Mrs. Tuggle."

At Nottoway Court House was situated the home of Hon. William Hodges Mann, the only Governor of Virginia from Nottoway. Judge Mann was not born in the county, but lived here most of his life, and the people of Nottoway are proud to call him their son. He was born at Williamsburg, Virginia, in 1843 and educated in a private school in Rockbridge County. He had no college education, but read law while employed in the Clerk's Office.

He practiced law in Nottoway until he was made the first Judge of the county, and served on the bench for twenty-two years. In 1899 he was elected to the State Senate and it was during this time that he was the author of two bills, for which the people of Virginia should ever be grateful to him. The Mann law of 1906 closed eight hundred rural saloons, and made Virginia dry except in the cities; and his loan bill, which aided in the erection of three hundred and fifty high schools in the State.

Judge Mann in 1905 ran for Governor of Virginia, but was defeated by Claude Swanson. Four years later in 1909, he again ran, and this time he was successful, defeating Harry St. George Tucker.

During his administration as Governor of Virginia occurred the famous Allen trials. As will be recalled, they were tried for the murder of Judge Massie and several members of his court, killed during a trial of one of their number for a minor offense.

Floyd and Claude Allen were given the death penalty, and although a great deal of pressure was brought to bear on Governor Mann to exercise executive clemency, he refused to take any action. His refusal to interfere with the court decisions in these cases is an example worthy of emulation by other governors.

Judge Mann was married twice. His first wife was Sallie Fitzgerald of Nottoway, and his second, Etta Donnan of Petersburg, Virginia.

He died in Petersburg, Virginia, in his eighty-fourth year.

BLENDON. Situated at Nottoway Court House was the seat of the Campbells in Nottoway. Tradition says they were descended from the Duke of Argyle in Scotland. Major Colin Campbell was the immigrant ancestor who came to Virginia and settled first in Northumberland County, and later on moved to Surry. He married August 22, 1741, Mary Gaskins, a descendant of Thomas Gaskin (1601-1665) of England and Northumberland County, Virginia. Major Colin Campbell, the immigrant, died April 7, 1780, in the 73rd year of his age. He had only two children, Elizabeth, who died an infant, and Dr. Archiball Campbell of Surry, born February 19, 1743, and died May 5, 1785.

Dr. Archiball Campbell married first, December, 1771, Mary Kendall Lee, daughter of Kendall Lee of Ditchley in Northumberland County. By this marriage he had four children: Colin; Mary Lee, who married Travis Harris; Archiball and William Lee Campbell. Next he married March 25, 1779, Elizabeth Harris, born October 14th, 1759, daughter of William and Frances Harris of Surry, and by this marriage he had four children, Thomas Campbell, born January 8, 1780, Frances Harris Campbell, born August 19, 1781, who was the second wife of Major John Epes of The Old Place in Nottoway, Wilmuth Campbell, born June 17, 1783, and Dr. Archiball Algernon Campbell, born October 31, 1785, and died October 31, 1865, who married first November 20, 1811, Sarah Epes (born March 23, 1793,

THE CASTLE

(Rear view) Built by Francis Fitzgerald.

and died November 26, 1833) daughter of Colonel Freeman Epes and Jane Wynn, and second, September 25, 1850, Martha Epes, sister of Sarah the first wife, and widow of Peter Branch Jones. There were no children by the last marriage.

We do not know definitely whether or not old Dr. Campbell of Surry, who married the second time Elizabeth Harris, ever settled in Nottoway, nor can we say with certainty who built Blendon. His wife, Elizabeth Harris, was the sister of Mrs. James Jones, of Mountain Hall, and of Mrs. James Fletcher of Somerset. She later married Major Richard Jones of The Poplars.

His son, Dr. Archiball Algernon Campbell, lived at Blendon. After his first wife died, Dr. Archiball Algernon Campbell wished to marry his first wife's sister, Martha. This was contrary to the old English, and also, the Virginia law at that time, which forbade a man to marry his deceased wife's sister, and so the couple were planning an elopement, when Dr. Campbell's son, Thomas Harris Campbell, who was a member of the legislature, asked his father to wait a few months until the legislature convened. He promised to have the law repealed, which he did, and acted as his father's best man at the wedding.

Dr. Archiball Algernon Campbell was a prominent physician and practiced his profession in the county for many years. He it was who made the stirring speech in behalf of secession at Nottoway Court House on April 7, 1861. His son,

Dr. Algernon Epes Campbell, who married Eleanor Jones May 16th, 1854, daughter of Captain Richard Jones of Bellefonte, later lived at Blendon. The original house consisted of only the central unit. The wings were later added, as was also the long porch. It remained in the Campbell family until about 1865 when it came into possession of a Mr. Simonds, who sold it about 1872 to George Dunn from Yorkshire, England. The Dunns lived here until 1910 when it passed to other hands and later the house was burned.

THE OAKS, across the road from Blendon was built by Dr. Campbell for his son, Thomas Harris Campbell, who married Fannie Pryor, a daughter of Dr. Theodorick Pryor. Thomas Campbell was a prominent lawyer, and was elected to the legislature when only twenty-one years of age. He was the second president of the Southside Railroad, now the Norfolk and Western, and was the father of Judge Archiball Campbell of Wytheville, Virginia.

Mrs. Fannie Campbell Wilson, a daughter of Thomas Harris Campbell, who now lives in Lexington, Virginia, relates a true incident of the Civil War period.

Her father lost his mother when quite young and his sister, Martha, with the help of a trusted servant "Mammy Sallie" cared for him. Tom Campbell's playmate was Mammy Sallie's son, Bob. The boys grew up together and when Tom went to William and Mary College, Bob accompanied him as his body servant. When Tom married and went to live at The Oaks, which his father had built for him, Bob was given him also, and became a trusted servant.

On account of weak lungs, Mr. Campbell did not serve in the army, but was appointed by the Confederate government to look after the confiscation of Federal property within the bounds of the Confederacy.

When the news came that Wilson's raid was coming through Nottoway, Mr. Campbell had Bob and Griffin, his servants, pack several trunks of valuables and hide them in "The Horse Trough" woods nearby.

When the raiders came, Bob in a moment of weakness, was persuaded by the Yankees to tell where the valuables were hidden, and also where his master was.

He took them to the trunks, but fortunately Mr. Campbell was not found. Soon the Confederates came and the raiders were driven back.

Bob was found hiding in the woods and was arrested, tried for his treachery and sentenced to be hanged. Greatly distressed, Mr. Campbell at once went to Richmond to see the Governor, seeking a full pardon for Bob. This the Governor refused to grant.

At the trial, Mr. Campbell himself conducted the defense, and in his closing speech he said, "Robert, I have tried to save you. I have done my best, Robert. I love you, Robert, Robert, goodbye."

The day Bob was executed, so great was Mr. Campbell's distress that he left home.

In later years Copeland Epes, whose wife was Mary Harrison, of Brunswick County, Virginia, lived at The Oaks.

THE POPLARS, one and a half miles north of Blendon, was one of the oldest settlements in Nottoway County, then Amelia, and was the seat of the Jones family. Major Richard Jones who lived here was the son of Richard Jones and was of Welsh decent. According to tradition he was of the same family as the Peter Jones who opened a trading station with the Indians at Peter's Point, which place was later called Petersburg. Major Jones was married three times. His first wife was Mary Robertson, of Amelia. Dr. James Jones, of Mountain Hall, was a son by this marriage.

His second wife was the widow Nicholson, nee Fletcher, a sister of Captain James Fletcher of Somerset. There were two sons by this marriage, Captain Richard Jones of Bellefonte and Nathan Jones. His third wife was the widow Campbell of Blendon, nee Harris. There was one child, a daughter, by this marriage, Elizabeth Harris Jones, who married Dr. George S. G. Bacon. Many of the Jones and Campbell family are buried in the old burying ground at The Poplars.

BLENDON

The seat of the Campbells in Nottoway, later the home of
the Dunns

OAK MOTTE is on the road from Nottoway Court House to Crewe built by Francis Epes of Lunenburg County, whose wife was Sally Williams. He built the house for his daughter, Mary Elizabeth Poythress Epes, who married Putnam Stith. Francis Epes of Lunenburg was a son of Colonel Peter Epes of High Peak in Prince George County, and was a member of the House of Delegates from Lunenburg County 1798-1800.

Putnam Stith was the son of Major John Stith, an officer of the Revolution who served on Lafayette's staff. His mother was Anne Washington, daughter of Lawrence Washington of Chotank, King George County. Lawrence Washington, of Chotank, was a cousin of General George Washington. Putnam Stith was also a kinsman of William Stith, the historian, one of the early presidents of William and Mary College, and a brother of Mrs. William Blunt Irby of Pleasant Hill.

His son, Putnam Stith, known to nearly everyone in the county as "Cousin Put", served in Company E, 12th Virginia Regiment, Mahone's Brigade, during the Civil War, and died in Petersburg, where he is buried in Blandford Cemetery.

HENDERSONVILLE, on the Nottoway Court House road, was built by James Henderson, a Scotchman, about the latter part of 1700, and was one of the oldest settlements in the county. James Henderson married Mary Marshall Booker.

He was a merchant and very well-to-do. A devout churchman, he helped to organize the first Presbyterian Church in the county. He lived in Nottoway for sixty years and died on November 8, 1817, age eighty years. He is buried between the railroad and the county road in what at that time was the garden. His wife, who died in 1829, and Isaac Oliver are also buried here. The Court House was once located at Hendersonville and later moved to its present location. James Henderson Fitzgerald, a member of the House of Delegates from Amelia County, inherited the Henderson estate. He was very wealthy, spending much of his time in Paris where he died.

Peter Epes, who married Martha Oliver, moved from Walnut Hill to Hendersonville after he sold Walnut Hill, intending to go South. His death from pneumonia prevented his going South, and his family continued to live at Hendersonville. Later, Dr. Algernon Epes Campbell, whose wife was Eleanor Jones, lived here.

THE GLEBE, near Hendersonville, was the home of Dr. George Fitzgerald, a son of Francis Fitzgerald, who served the county as clerk for many years. Dr. Fitzgerald married three times. His first wife was Susan F. Thweatt, whom he married May 19, 1831, and by this marriage he had one son, Edmond.

His second wife was Catherine Frances Campbell, a daughter of Dr. A. A. Campbell of Blendon. His son by this marriage, Colonel John

Patterson Fitzgerald of Farmville, Virginia, married Floreda Flournoy of Prince Edward County.

His third wife was Sallie Tazewell. By this marriage he had the following children: Mary Louisa, who married Mr. Pierce of Richmond; Tazewell, who married Miss Doggett, a daughter of Bishop Doggett and later died in Richmond; Littleton, who married Alice Flournoy of Prince Edward; and a daughter, Page.

SUNNYSIDE was early a Balwin settlement and is near Hendersonville. This was the home of Clerk Dick Epes, who married Agnes Batte. Sidney P. Epes, who served the Fourth District in Congress, was born here August 20, 1865.

MICA HILL, just east of Crewe, was settled by Captain P. O. Lipscomb, whose wife was Mary Hardaway. Their children were, Mrs. Sidney Graves, Mrs. Hudgins and Mrs. Rowlett Perkinson.

ELEVEN OAKS, also known as Robertson's Tavern, was situated just on the outskirts of Crewe, on the old road to Nottoway Court House. John Robertson, whose wife was Sarah Jennings, daughter of William Jennings of Jennings Ordinary, was the first Robertson to live here of whom we have any record. His son, William Archer I, known as "Lame Archer", next lived here, whose wife was Nancy Knight. Their children were,

Eliza; Martha, who married Major Hezekiah Anderson; John Archer, of Rock Castle; James, Mary, Malloy and William Archer II. William Archer Robertson II married Eliza Davis, daughter of Dr. John Davis and Eliza Durant of Violet Bank, near Petersburg, and lived at Eleven Oaks until the house was burned by Yankee soldiers, during the latter part of the war. He then moved to Hollywood across the road from Eleven Oaks. His son, William Archer III married Elizabeth Henry Southall, and lived at Nottoway Court House until his death.

BACON'S HALL, to the north of Crewe and almost in sight, was the home of Colonel Tyree G. Bacon. Colonel Bacon was a veteran of the War of 1812, and served in the General Assembly of Virginia, session 1832. His son, Dr. George S. G. Bacon, who lived in Mecklenburg County, married Elizabeth Harris Jones, a daughter of Major Richard Jones of The Poplars. Dr. Bacon it was whe killed Dr. John S. Hardaway in the duel at Nottoway Court House in 1818.

Dr. Bacon himself was severely wounded by Dr. Hardaway, and is said to have died from the effect of his wounds.

Colonel Tyree Bacon's daughter, Mary J. C. Bacon, married Jesse H. Leath, March 22, 1832, and Colonel Bacon gave Bacon's Hall to her after her marriage. By this marriage there were eight children, five sons and three daughters: James,

Branch, Tyree, Joseph, George William, Virginia, Harriett and Sarah. All five of the sons served in Company C, 18th Virginia Pickett's division, and one of the sons, Tyree Glenn Bacon Leath, was lieutenant of the Company. All five received wounds during the war.

Lieutenant Leath was wounded at Fraser's Farm on June 20, 1862. He was incapacitated for active service because of this wound and was made chief enrolling officer for Nottoway County until April 4, 1865, when he was met by Sheridan's Scouts and shot through the body. He never fully recovered from the effect of this wound, and died in May, 1875.

At the outbreak of the War, Lieutenant Leath was presented with a silver handled sword by the ladies of Nottoway County.

Bacon Hall later was the home of George William Lamkin Leath, a son of Jesse H. Leath and Mary J. C. Bacon Leath. He married Laurel H. Vaughan, a daughter of Jesse Nelson Vaughan. George William Lamkin Leath died June 29, 1922, the last of his generation.

ROCK CASTLE. On the northern outskirts of Crewe stands an old house known as Rock Castle, once the home of the Robertson family. Soon after the war, Dr. A. Dimmick of Pennsylvania lived here.

Dr. Dimmick was a friend of B. F. Williams, also of Pennsylvania, and persuaded his friend, Williams, whose health at the time was bad, to come South. In 1876 B. F. Williams came to Nottoway from Pennsylvania and lived for some time at Rock Castle.

Unlike most Northerners who came South after the war, Mr. Williams seemed to have had the State of his adoption at heart. He soon took an interest in local politics, and was elected to the State Senate on the Republican ticket from Nottoway. It was about this time that the Readjuster movement began.

The leader of this movement, General William Mahone, sought to build up a vast patronage that could be used to make Virginia permanently Republican, but to do this, he had to control the legislature. He sought to bind all the Readjusters to support the decision of the Readjuster Caucus.

In the House, Mahone had a majority and could carry out his plan. In the Senate, however, there were four who refused to sign the pledge to enter the Caucus, and to accept its decisions. These men were Samuel H. Newberry of Bland, Peyton G. Hale of Grayson, A. M. Lybrook of Patrick, and B. F. Williams of Nottoway. Parson Massie, having turned against Mahone on account of his failure to receive the appointment of Auditor of Public Accounts, alligned himself with these four Senators.

On the vote of these men, the fate of the State depended. If they stood with Mahone, Virginia would be looted, and if they rebelled, the State would be saved. So much depended on their vote, that these Senators came to be known as the "Big Four". Every conceivable pressure was brought to bear by the Mahone faction to have them vote with the Readjusters.

When Mahone's patronage bills came up, the four with Parson Massey courageously voted with the Democrats against the Readjusters, which gave the Democrats a majority of six.

It was almost as narrow an escape as Virginia had in 1869, when the Republican Carpet-Baggers and the Scallywags sought to create a Republican Solid South, and by their infamies made it solidly Democratic. The State of Virginia has recently recognized the valuable services of these men and a portrait of the "Big Four" with Parson Massey, painted by the young Richmond artist, Silvette, has been hung on the walls of the Senate Chamber in the State Capitol.

HEATH COURT is located one mile northwest of Crewe on the Old Burkeville road, and was the home of Littleberry Royal, who lived there in 1827. It was later the home of Louis Countesse Bouldin, who came to Nottoway from Charlotte and married Catherine Cralle Ward, a daughter of Benjamin Ward of West Creek. He had two brothers who served in Congress. Thomas Tyler Bouldin succeeded John Randolph and James Wood Bouldin succeeded his brother, Thomas Tyler Bouldin. James Wood Bouldin was the father of Mrs. Louis Bouldin Spencer, the mother of Mrs. Theodorick Pryor Epes.

Louis Countesse Bouldin lived at Heath's Court in 1862.

IVERNESS is located half way between Crewe and Burkeville, a fine old Colonial mansion with large white columns. The house sits in a beautiful grove of oaks, sycamores and other trees some distance from the road. The first owner seems to have been a man by the name of Jeter, who probably patented the land. In 1792 Richard Broddus married Maria Jeter and inherited the property.

In 1800 Broddus sold Iverness to Thomas Dickinson, who built the present house and gave it to his nephew, Robert Dickinson, who married a Miss Dupuy of Poplar Grove at Jennings Ordinary. Colonel Purnell Dickinson, who afterwards lived at Roseland, and Judge Asa Dickinson were both born here; also Clem Dickinson, who is now a member of Congress from Missouri, although well over eighty years old. He was at Inverness in 1864 while the battle of The Crater was in progress, and told Judge Walter Watson that the firing of the guns could be distinctly heard. The distance from Inverness to The Crater battlefield is fifty miles.

Bettie Dickinson, who married Colonel W. C. Knight of Inwood, lived here before her marriage to Colonel Knight. In 1869 Colonel McLean bought the plantation and named it Inverness for the house of McLean in Scotland. Later Perkins Agnew, who married Helen McLean,

INVERNESS

Built by Thomas Dickinson, about 1800, now the home of
Stuart Agnew.

bought it and his son, Stuart Agnew, who married Elizabeth Bostick, now lives here.

MALVERN HILL, adjoining Inverness, was the home of the family of Sam Royall, whose wife after his death moved to Malvern Hill before the Civil War. His children were: Thomas E. Royall, who married Miss Hubbard of Alabama and who was Superintendent of Schools in the county for a long time; Dr. Willie Royall, a Methodist preacher; Carrie Royall, who married Dr. Warriner; Lucy, who married T. N. Beck, a Methodist minister; Matilda, who married Dr. Trent of Goochland County; and Florence, who married Mr. Acree of Lynchburg.

FOREST GROVE is about two miles north of Burkeville. Dr. Dupuy, a brother of John Dupuy, first owned this place and later it was a Robertson settlement. Henry I. Robertson, who married Eliza Fowlkes, once lived here. On the lawn are some of the biggest oaks to be seen anywhere, one tree measuring seventeen and one-half feet around. Joe Vaughan, who married Ida Hillsman, now lives at Forrest Grove.

MILLER'S HILL, built prior to 1833, standing on the highest elevation between Richmond and Danville, is near Burkeville and was built by Anderson Perkins Miller, who married first Martha Perkinson of Prince Edward County. They had four daughters: Martha Anne, who married Dr.

James Agnew and lived at Roseland in Prince Edward County; Jane Maria, who married a Mr. Hudson; Eliza Armstead, who married William Ward of "West Creek"; and Mary Anderson, who married a Jones. Anderson Perkins Miller next married a widow, Sarah Nash, nee Thweatt, who lived near Hampden-Sydney. By this marriage he had four children: Capt. Giles A .Miller, who married Jane Webster and lived at Grape Lawn; Henry T., who lived in Chesterfield County; Sarah Barksdale, who never married; and Anderson Perkins Miller, Jr. Anderson Perkins Miller, Jr., first married E. M. J. Willson. By this union there were two children, both of whom died young. His second wife was Mary Scott, daughter of Dr. George Scott of Amelia County. There were two children by this marriage: Annie Perkins Miller and Sallie Thweatt Miller, who married T. O. Sandy. Mrs. T. O. Sandy inherited Miller's Hall and now lives there.

GRAPE LAWN, near Burkeville, is just across the line in Prince Edward County. This was the home of Dr. Giles A. Miller, whose first wife was Jane Webster. Their children were: Henry T., Anthony W. (Captain Tony), and Polk Miller of Richmond; Giles A., Jr.; Mollie, who married Charles Crump; Alice, who first married Major Tom Friend Willson, and later married Harvey Wily, Perkins, and Rosa. Captain Tony, Polk and Henry T. all served in the Civil War. Dr.

Giles Miller later married Mattie Sloan and had two daughters, Zena and Emogen.

Tony Miller had the unusual distinction of having seen active service in two wars, the Civil and Spanish-American. His service in the Confederate Army began when as a mere youth he was mustered in as a private in Troop G of the First Virginia Cavalry at Ashland, May 19, 1861, known as "The Amelia Troop."

In the Spanish-American War he served as a second lieutenant in Company B, First Virginia Regiment, from April 8, 1896 until transferred to Company B, Second Virginia Volunteers. In May, 1898, he was promoted to first lieutenant and later was made captain of Company B, Seventieth Infantry Virginia Volunteers. Captain Tony Miller married Miss Fannie Hatchett, a daughter of Captain William E. Hatchett, of Lunenburg County, who was a distinguished officer in the Confederate service. Captain Miller's grandfather, Colonel Anthony Webster, was a gallant officer of the Revolutionary War.

BURKE'S OLD TAVERN. A short distance southwest of Burkeville is Burke's Old Tavern, built about 1731 by the father of Colonel Richard Burke, from whose family Burkeville later derived its name.

The builder of the tavern was a salt merchant, and lived in Norfolk before coming to Nottoway. His son, Colonel Richard Burke, first married a Miss Leigh from Prince Edward, and his second wife was a Miss Ligon. The old tavern has housed many famous guests, among them John Randolph of Roanoke. The stage road ran by here to Richmond. The original house is still standing and is owned by W. B. Farrar, who married Miss Leath.

GLENMORE is on the old road between Burkeville and Jennings Ordinary. This was originally a Watson settlement, and the land was patented by William Watson. The old Watson burying ground is located here. Later Dr. William H. Robertson, who married Rebecca Shore, a daughter of Dr. Robert Shore, moved to Glenmore from Amelia. They had the following children: Shore, who married Lizzie Cralle; William H., who married Nannie Robinson; Walter, who married Lelia Eggleston; Beverly, who married Miss Baird; Lillie, who married Samuel Chamberlain; and Ivanhoe, who never married.

LOCUST GROVE is about two and a half miles south of Burkeville, and is one of the oldest houses in the county still standing. It was built about 1807 by Lew Jones, who married Prudence Ward in 1796. He named the place Locust Grove after the old Jones home in Lunenburg County, and afterwards sold it to A. C. Barton, who lived here for a number of years. A. C. Barton was married twice; his first wife was Elizabeth Cary and his second Jane Ellett. Lew Jones was a great

MILLER'S HILL

Built by Anderson Perkins Miller prior to 1833, now the
home of Mrs. T. O. Sandy.

friend of A. C. Barton, and often came back to Locust Grove to visit. On one of these visits he presented Mrs. Barton with two immense cases of silver ware. Just before General Lee surrendered, when word came that the Yankees were coming, Mrs. Barton took all her silver, hams and other valuables and hid them in the attic. Soon the Yankees came, and running true to form, they began to search the house. They took everything of value they could find, including the silver. They were, however, considerate enough to leave the empty cases behind, which are still in the possession of the family—a grim reminder of the vandalism of Yankee troops. This old house has some beautiful mantels and paneling. Mrs. Dugans, the present owner, was recently offered five hundred dollars for the paneling in one room.

JENNINGS ORDINARY. Near here were some of the finest homes in Nottoway before the war.

The place was first settled by Colonel William Jennings who was born in England and died in Amelia, now Nottoway County, in 1775. The house in which Colonel Jennings lived is still standing, an old tavern from which Jennings Ordinary received its name.

Colonel Jennings married Mary Jane Pulliam of Hanover County in 1724. He is supposed to have been the heir to the Jennings fortune about which there has been so much litigation in recent years.

It seems that in 1798 William Jennings, of Acton, Suffolk and Grosvenor Square, London, the only child of Robert Jennings and Anne Gpidote, died in England a bachelor at the age of ninety-seven. This William Jennings was a nephew of Colonel William Jennings of Nottoway. He left a fortune consisting of real estate and personal property valued at two million pounds sterling, and is said to have left it to the heirs of Colonel William Jennings of Nottoway. Colonel Jennings' heirs were not located at the time, and the real estate passed to George Augustus Curzon, and thence to Earl Howe, while the personal property passed to Lady Andover and William Ligon, and has remained in possession of their heirs since that time. In later years there have been several attempts made by the heirs of Colonel William Jennings to dispossess the present owners of this estate, but so far the courts have found in favor of the defendants.

Other Jennings homes in the county are Mallory Hill,, Rural Retreat, and Hico.

MALLORY HILL, the home of Macajah Jennings, built about 1807 and still standing, is now owned by Gordon Lee Jennings, a descendant of Colonel William Jennings. Mallory Hill has been in the hands of the Jennings family continuously.

RURAL RETREAT, built about 1790 and afterwards about 1840, bought by Captain John Fowlkes, himself a descendant of Colonel William Jennings, is now owned by a daughter of Captain Fowlkes, Mrs. Amanda Lipscomb, the oldest living descendant of Colonel William Jennings.

HICO was built about 1841 by Macajah Childs Jennings, a great grandson of Colonel William Jennings.

CEDAR GROVE at Jennings Ordinary, was first a Dupuy, then an Eggleston settlement. Captain Bob Shore, whose wife was Mollie Eggleston, lived here. Miss Georgena Epes taught school here for some time.

POPLAR GROVE, near the Ordinary, was the first Dupuy settlement in the county. The Dupuys were of French Huguenot ancestry. Captain James Dupuy, born May 5, 1758, and died June 30, 1823, was an officer of the Revolutionary War. He married Mary Purnell, born March 13, 1763, and died February 28, 1828. Poplar Grove was later a Fowlkes settlement. The old Dupuy burying ground is located here.

MOUNTAIN HALL, built soon after the Revolutionary War by Dr. James Jones, about three miles northeast of Crewe, is one of the handsomest homes in the county. The house stands on a pleasing elevation overlooking Deep Creek, and is of the Georgian type.

It is not in sight of the main road, but is approached down a long lane of the most enormous cedars to be found anywhere. One instinctively thinks of the cedars of Lebanon while passing through this beautiful driveway. On the lawn too are many handsome trees of cedar, magnolia, box and other varieties. One cedar tree at the corner of the house is so large that two people with arms outstretched can scarcely meet around it. Some of the shrubs are very rare and are said to have been imported from Scotland.

The house is square and two-storied. The lower part is of red brick and the walls four feet thick, while the upper story is frame, with large clapboards fastened on with wrought nails.

The front porch which is to one side is of Colonial type, with arched ceiling and slender columns. From the porch one enters the house through a doorway of lovely design with double panels and fan-shaped leaded glass. The hallway is spacious and inviting, running the entire length of the house.

All of the rooms have mantels of rare carving, with large open fireplaces. The windows are very deep and large enough to be used as seats.

Dr. James Jones, who built the house, was a son of Major Richard Jones of The Poplars. He married Catherine Harris of Surry County, who was a sister of Mrs. Campbell of Blendon, and also Mrs. Fletcher of Somerset. Dr. Jones was one of the most prominent men in Southside Virginia, and certainly one of Nottoway's most illustrious sons.

BURKE'S OLD TAVERN

Built about 1731, now the home of W. B. Farrar.

He served in Congress for a number of years, was Hospital Surgeon General during the War of 1812, and an outstanding physician. His parents were very wealthy and gave him the benefit of a splendid education.

He was graduated from Hampden-Sydney College in 1791, and later attended the University of Pennsylvania. From the University of Pennsylvania he repaired to the University of Edinburgh in Scotland, at that time the principal center of medical learning in Europe, where he was graduated with high honors. Returning to his native State and county, his education and talents soon placed him at the head of his profession.

While in Europe he became imbued with the false doctrines of the day, of free thought and infidel philosophy, and became one of the prominent members of the "Tom Paine Infidel Club", a society organized in Amelia County near Paineville. He continued his membership in this society until the death of his only daughter, a beautiful girl of eleven years, to whom he was very devoted, and whose death turned his thoughts to religion, from which he could only find comfort in his sorrow.

After the death of his daughter he became an elder and pillar in the Presbyterian church. He assembled his infidel club, and delivered before it such a Christian address that it at once disbanded and never met again.

The pathetic inscription on the slab covering the graves of his two daughters bears witness to his devotion to his children and his great grief at their death. The inscription reads as follows:

"In memory of two lovely daughters of James and Catherine Jones, Mary Frances, born July 4, 1798, died October 31, 1799, and Maria Anne, born December 24, 1799, died November 24, 1810. Humbly resigned to the will of God who gave and who hath taken away, the bereaved parents have placed this mounmental marble to commemorate the early virtues and the dawning beauties of their departed offspring, which to them were a presage of an abundant harvest of earthly joy and of earthly bliss."

Dr. Jones was opposed to slavery, and although a large slave owner, he made ample provision in his will for the manumission of his slaves and the emigration to Liberia of as many as desired to go. This clause in his will reads as follows: "The whole subject is to be fully and intelligently presented to their minds, so they may have the option of going to the Colony or remaining in bondage. And I particularly desire that any of them who may be willing to go, shall at any time be emancipated by due form of law by my executors, and transferred to such agents of said Colony as may be willing to receive them."

After his death in 1848, Dr. Jones' wife immediately began to carry out the provisions of his will, and tendered to the slaves in the spring of 1849 the privilege of going to Liberia, and to those that desired to remain after receiving their freedom, she granted their request in so far as the laws of the State of Virginia permitted. Dr. Jones' **anti-slave** convictions were well-known, yet in a community which was the stronghold of slavery, he was kept in Congress by his constituents, showing in what high esteem and regard he was held by the people of the district.

While in Congress his family had influential social connections with President Monroe and others of high office. In their home Dr. Wm. S. White, who lived at Mountain Hall when he first came to Nottoway to begin his pastorate, said: "They were among the most highly cultivated persons in this or any other country. Their beautiful home was literally the abode of the most refined intelligent piety, and the resort of many visitors likeminded with themselves."

Dr. Jones died at Mountain Hall in his seventy-sixth year, and is buried in the old grave yard in the garden. Probably no higher tribute could be paid him than is written on his tomb placed over his grave by his wife, but said to have been composed by Benjamin Watkins Leigh, U. S. Senator from Virginia, and reads as follows:

"Sacred to the memory of James Jones, M. D., graduate of the University of Edinburgh, born 11th December, 1772, died 25th April, 1848.

A man whose character none can contemplate without admiration, or admire without profit. A statesman honored for his talents, erudition and patriotism. A Christian deeply imbued with the spirit of the gospel. In the closing scene of life he exhibited the humble, tranquil submission which religion inspires. His devoted wife erects this frail memorial to his virtues."

After Dr. Jones' death, Mountain Hall changed hands a good many times. In later years just after the Civil War, Colonel Calvin Jeffress sold Woodville and bought Mountain Hall, where he spent his declining years, and where he is buried near the Jones grave yard in the garden. Colonel Jeffress commanded the Jeffress Battery during the Civil War. His son, Thornton Jeffress, afterwards sold Mountain Hall. It is now owned by H. E. Rorer, who has done much to restore this old home.

ANDERSON HOME. Adjoining Mountain Hall and the Harry Dyson place, on the Mountain Hall road, was the home of Major Hezekiah Anderson, who married Martha Robertson, a daughter of Archer Robertson of **Eleven Oaks**, also known as Robertson's Tavern. Eleven Oaks was located just on the outskirts of what is now the town of Crewe on the old road to Nottoway Court House. Major Anderson was a prominent man in the county, and at one time president of the Bellefonte Jocky Club. He died from the effects of a fall from his horse.

MOUNTAIN HALL

Built soon after the Revolutionary War by Dr. James Jones,
later the home of Colonel Calvin Jeffress, now the home of
H. E. Rorer.

He was the father of Mary Jane Anderson, the mother of the famous Southern poet, Sidney Lanier.

The sessional record of the Presbyterian Church of Nottoway County bears the following entries, as copied by Mrs. R. F. Dillard:

"On June 18th, 1832, the following were Baptized: Emily, William Henry, Mary Jane (Mrs. Lanier) Halbert, Melville and Waverly Anderson." William Henry Anderson, a graduate of Hampden-Sydney in 1839, and a brilliant lawyer, died in Georgia. He once taught school in the county and was the subject of "Jonny Reb's" sketch, "The Old Field School", by F. R. Farrar. His brother, Hon. Clifford Anderson, was a distinguished member of the Macon, Georgia, bar.

WOODLAND, near Jennings Ordinary, was once a Dupuy settlement, and later the home of the Watsons. The early ancestors of the Watsons came from England and Wales. Robert A. Watson, who married his cousin, Mary Elizabeth Watson. moved to Nottoway in 1852 from Lunenburg County and purchased Woodland from John Dupuy.

His son, Meredith Watson, who married Josephine Robertson, was living at Woodland at the outbreak of the Civil War. Colonel Watson, who was appointed by Thomas Jefferson in 1780 lieutenant of a company of militia in Prince Edward County, made captain in 1782 and later in

1803 made colonel, and who fought in the battles of Camden and Guilford Court House, was the grandfather of Meredith Watson.

Meredith and Josephine Watson had thirteen children, six of whom are now living. Leon who never married, Hunter who married Pattie Epes, a daughter of Judge Branch Epes of Gatewood in Dinwiddie County, Fannie A. who married Dr. J. H. C. Winston of Hampden-Sydney College, Lois, who married Hilary H. Royal, captain United States Navy, Rebecca Shore, who married Judge F. T. Sutton, Jr., and Calva H., who married Percy W. Wootton.

Meredith Watson was a member of Company E, 3rd Virginia Cavalry during the Civil War. His son, Walter Allen Watson, who married Constance Tinsley January 18, 1905, was an outstanding man in the community. He was greatly beloved, and did as much for the Fourth District perhaps as any man who ever lived in it. Educated at Hampden-Sydney College and graduated in law from the University of Virginia, he began the practice of law in Nottoway in 1889 at the age of twenty-two. Two years later when only twenty-four, he was a member of the Virginia Senate, the youngest member of that body.

On June 6, 1895, when only twenty-eight, he was elected Commonwealth's Attorney of Nottoway and served in that capacity until elected judge. In 1901-02 the State of Virginia called a Constitutional Convention, and Mr. Watson was elected a delegate from Nottoway and Amelia, one of the youngest members of the Convention, being less than thirty-four years of age. He at once took, and was gladly conceded by his associates, a commanding position in the Convention. He was particularly interested in having the election laws of the State changed. Through his efforts the Nottoway County Resolutions, prepared by him when he was Chairman of the Democratic Committee of his county, were brought before the Convention and had great weight in framing the election laws of the State. These resolutions set forth frankly and forcibly the dangers to the Democratic Party should the political methods used to maintain white supremacy be continued, and asked that the Convention provide an organic law that would legalize the elimination of the vicious and illiterate voter. His speech in behalf of his suffrage plan is justly regarded as a classic. In 1904 Mr. Watson was made judge of the Fourth Judicial Circuit, a position he filled with such credit as to attract nation-wide attention.

He resigned as judge in 1912 to offer for a seat in Congress, and was elected, serving through the Sixty-third, Sixty-fourth and Sixty-fifth, and was re-elected to the Sixty-sixth Congress without opposition. It was his intention not to offer for Congress again, but to retire to Woodland and write a history of Nottoway and Southside Virginia, a work he long had in mind, and for which he had collected much data. His untimely death on December 24, 1919, while a member of Congress cut short his work in this direction.

Mr. Watson was a man of many lovable traits and of a delightful personality. His courtesy of manner and his conversation were typical of an earlier generation. He seemed never to forget the names and faces of people he met, and could usually tell from what county and what part of the State they came. Perhaps no finer tribute could be paid anyone than was paid Judge Watson by his friends, Judge R. G. Southall, who succeeded him as judge, and George Keith Taylor, Commonwealth Attorney of Amelia County in an appreciation of him written after his death. They said: "He will long be remembered as a just, merciful and able judge, a distinguished citizen, a faithful and affectionate friend, and one who by his many virtues, brilliancy and charming characteristics adorned his day and time."

Adjoining Woodland was the home of Dr. Benjamin Royall, a brother-in-law of Mrs. Sam Royall of Malvern Hill. It was here that Major Hezekiah Anderson was living when he met with the accident that caused his death. He either fell or was thrown from his horse, and was found in the woods in a dying condition.

THE OLD HOMESTEAD, the home of Crawley Jones, who married first, Mary Campbell and second, Catherine Jones, is located on what is known as the Chair road between Jennings Ordin-

WOODLAND

First a Dupuy settlement, later the home of the Watsons.

ary and West Creek. It was afterwards known as the Burke Place.

THE HERMITAGE is on the Namozine road not far from Fergusonville. William Jones, a brother of Crawley Jones, lived here. He married Pattie Scott Agnew.

LINWOOD is also on the Namozine road and was the home of Captain Baxter Jones, whose wife was Fannie Dyson. Baxter Jones was first lieutenant of Company E, 3rd Virginia Cavalry, and commanded the company most of the latter part of the war. He was generally called "Captain".

BRIGHT SHADOWS, about three miles from Jennings Ordinary, was built by Robert Beverley who married Virginia Epes McCormick. He was the son of Harry Standard Beverley and Frances Susan Doswell.

After he built the house, he gave the biggest party, it is said, that was ever held in the county. He had the best caterer he could get from Richmond, and Josh Motley, his servant, who was a noted fiddler, and who afterwards played for General Stuart in the army, helped furnish the music.

Bob Beverley was a great wit, and many of his sayings are still repeated by the people of the county.

He was once a devoted admirer of a lady who lived in Dinwiddie County, who had many suitors, each trying to get ahead of the others. One of the suitors, came to take her out driving one day with his horses hitched tandem thinking, thereby to carry off the honors. Not to be outdone, Mr. Beverley the next time drove up with a coachman, a footman, and a coach and four. After the war he moved to Nottoway Court House, and later John E. Perkinson, whose wife was Virginia Williams, a daughter of David G. Williams, lived at Bright Shadows.

OLDEN PLACE, thought to have been built by a man named Dalby about 1781, six miles from the Ordinary, was the old Wily home. This was first a Webster settlement, and later Colonel Crump, whose wife was a Miss Miller, lived here. Still later, Harvey Wily, a veteran of the Civil War, who married the widow Willson, nee Miller, made it his home. Harvey Wily was a member of Second Virginia Cavalry, and at the battle of Five Forks, acted as courier for General William H. F. Lee, during this engagement receiving a wound from which he never fully recovered. Olden Place has an unusual stairway of walnut and some very old paneling. The place is now owned by J. S. Robertson, of Blackstone. Near by is the Sailor's Creek battlefield. Olden Place was used as a hospital after the battle of Sailor's Creek.

BELFAST was one of the first Fitzgerald settlements in the county and is not far from Fancy

Hill. Francis Fitzgerald, who lived here, was clerk of Nottoway County from November 7, 1805, to 1851-52. He was a man of the highest integrity and one of the most efficient clerks who ever served the county. He was an ardent Democrat and supporter of Andrew Jackson, but hated Henry Clay, whom he regarded as too great a compromiser. Francis Fitzgerald was the son of Captain William Fitzgerald of Leinster who served in the Revolutionary War. He married his cousin, Fanny Jones, a daughter of Daniel Jones of Mount Airy. There were ten children of this union, seven sons and three daughters.

His son, Charles Fitzgerald, later lived at Belfast. He married first Miss Hobson and they had the following children: Louisa, who married Edward S. Deane, Clerk of Nottoway County; Sallie, who married Hon. William Hodges Mann; Charles, who never married; and Anne, who became the second wife of Clerk Edward S. Deane.

Charles Fitzgerald's second wife was Rebecca Bland.

Rev. James Henderson Fitzgerald, of Buckingham County, was a son of Clerk Francis Fitzgerald and brother of Charles, as was also Dr. George Fitzgerald, who lived at the Glebe. Belfast was burned in 1866.

CHEVY CHASE or BEASLEYS, as it was called, which belonged to R. S. Epes of Poplar Hill, is also in this neighborhood. R. S. Epes married Fanny Dunn.

MOUNT AIRY was the home of Daniel Jones, who married first, a Miss Baker and second, the widow Ward, who was before her marriage Catherine Cralle, known as "the queen." She first married Colonel Benjamin Ward of West Creek and then Daniel Jones. Crawley Jones, who afterwards lived at the Homestead, was born at Mt. Airy.

BARE BONES. On the Namozine road between Jennings Ordinary and Fergusonville on Barebone Creek is a place called Bare Bones, which tradition says was the birthplace of Nancy Hanks, the mother of President Lincoln.

There are numerous records at Amelia Court House of the Hanks family, some with the same given names as those of the family of Lincoln's mother. Regardless of what Dr. Barton and other authorities on Lincoln may say, the records at Amelia Court House seem to bear out the tradition that Nancy Hanks was born at Barebones, at that time in Amelia, but now in Nottoway County.

BALDWINS, near the Amelia line, was the home of Dr. James Scott, who afterwards moved to Amelia County and built Scotland.

SOMERSET is on the Namozine road and is also near the Amelia line. This was the home of Captain James Fletcher, whose wife was Sallie

OLDEN PLACE

Near Sailor's Creek Battlefield, once a Webster settlement, later the Wily home.

Harris, a sister of Mrs. James Jones of Mountain Hall and of Mrs. Archibald Campbell of Blendon.

Captain Fletcher died June 27th, 1845, in his 74th year. His daughter, Martha Anne Fletcher, married Dr. John S. Hardaway, who was killed in the duel with Dr. George S. G. Bacon. It is said that Mrs. Hardaway never allowed the word "bacon" to be used in her presence, so painful was the recollection of the affair between her husband and Dr. Bacon. Her daughter, Jacqueline Segar Hardaway, by this marriage, married Thomas Freeman Epes of Windrow. Another daughter, Sally Anne, married her first cousin, Horace Hardaway, of Cedar Hill. Martha Anne Hardaway, nee Fletcher, afterwards married Dr. Robert Shore, and the children by this marriage were: R. E. Shore; Louise, who married Robert Ward; Rebecca, who married Dr. W. H. Robertson of Glenmore; and Elizabeth, who married Mr. Eggleston, and was the mother of Lelia Eggleston, who married her cousin, Walter H. Robertson.

Dr. John S. Hardaway died on July 4th, 1818, and is buried at Somerset.

Captain Fletcher's daughter, Mary Catherine Fletcher, married Matthew Myrick Harrison. Their son, Dr. Matthew Myrick Harrison, Jr., married Martha Anne Cuningham. Mary Catherine Harrison, a daughter of this union, married Copeland Epes of The Oaks in Nottoway.

SPRINGFIELD, near Somerset and just across the line in Amelia, was a Hardaway home. Amelia Court House was once located here.

WEST CREEK, about five miles northeast of Crewe, is the oldest Ward settlement in the County. Colonel Benjamin Ward, who married Catherine Cralle, "the queen," lived here. It was built sometime before the Revolutionary War, and burned April 12, 1902, while it was the home of George Verser. Other Ward homes are **Bellefield, Ingleside** and **Spring Grove.**

BELLEFIELD was the home of Benjamin Ward, Jr., a son of Colonel Benjamin Ward of West Creek and is situated about three miles from Jennings Ordinary on the Pulliam road. Benjamin Ward, Jr., married Sarah Fitzgerald, a daughter of Captain William Fitzgerald of Leinster. Many of the Ward and Fitzgerald families are buried at Bellefield.

INGLESIDE was the home of Robert Ward, who married Louise Shore, a daughter of Dr. Robert Shore. B. F. Williams of "The Big Four" moved from **Rockcastle** to Ingleside and ran a mill here.

SPRING GROVE is also near The Ordinary and was the home of William Ward, who married Martha Jones, a sister of Crawley Jones of The Homestead.

At West Creek took place that notable encounter between Peter Francisco, a soldier of the Revolution, and nine of Tarleton's Dragons, in which Peter Francisco, after being captured, wounded two and put to flight the rest. A vivid account of this is given in Howe's History of Virginia and is, in part, as follows:

"While the British Army was spreading havoc and desolation all around them by their plundering and burnings in Virginia in 1781, Francisco had been reconnoitering, and while stopping at the house of a Mr. Ward, then in Amelia, now Nottoway County, nine of Tarleton's Cavalry came up with three negroes, and told him he was their prisoner. Seeing he was overpowered by numbers, he made no resistance. Believing him to be very peacable they all went into the house, leaving him and the pay-master together. 'Give up all you possess of value,' said the latter, 'or prepare to die.' 'I have nothing to give up,' said Francisco, 'so use your pleasure.' 'Deliver instantly,' rejoined the soldier, 'those masse silver buckles which you wear in your shoes.' 'They were a present from a valued friend,' replied Francisco, 'and it would grieve me to part with them. Give them into your hands I never will. You have the power; take them if you think fit.' The soldier put his sabre under his arm, and bent down to take them. Francisco, finding so favorable an opportunity to recover his liberty, stepped one pace in the rear, drew the sword with force from under his arm, and instantly gave him a blow across the scull.

'My enemy,' observed Francisco, 'was brave, and, though severely wounded, drew a pistol, and in the same moment that he pulled the trigger, I cut his hand nearly off. The bullet grazed my side. One of the soldiers mounted the only horse he could get and presented his gun at my breast. It missed fire. I rushed on the muzzle of the gun. A short struggle ensued. I disarmed and wounded him. Tarleton's troop of four hundred were in sight. All was hurry and confusion, which I increased by repeatedly hollooing as loud as I could, 'Come on, my brave boys, now's your time; we will soon dispatch these few, and then attack the main body.'

The wounded man flew to the troop, and the others were panic-struck, and fled. The eight horses that were left behind I gave Ward to conceal for me. Discovering Tarleton had dispatched ten more in pursuit of me, I made off. I evaded their vigilance.

They stopped to refresh themselves. I, like an old fox, doubled, and fell on their rear. Finding my situation dangerous, and surrounded by enemies, I went off with my horses."

Peter Francisco lived in Buckingham County. After the Revolutionary War he was made sergeant-at-arms of the House of Delegates. He is buried in Shocco Cemetery in Richmond.

The daughters of the American Revolution have recently erected a tablet at West Creek to commemorate the valor of this brave man.

This brings to a close our effort to describe in some measure the old homes of Nottoway and the families that once occupied them. Most of the old places have long since fallen into decay, and the old people are now dead and gone. Their descendants, however, remain, and it behooves them to take a page from the book of the past, to emulate the many virtues and sterling qualities of those who have gone before, and thus uphold the traditions of a civilization that is also past, but whose like, the world has seldom, if ever, seen.

"Lord God of Hosts, be with us yet,
Lest we forget—lest we forget!"

[THE END]

www.ingramcontent.com/pod-product-compliance
Lightning Source LLC
Chambersburg PA
CBHW070921270326
41927CB00011B/2665